HOUSE PLANTS
CACTI AND SUCCULENTS

Perhaps few groups of plants have attracted more attention in recent years than house plants and cacti and succulents. The fact that all the plants in the first group and many in the second can be grown in ordinary room conditions has had much to do with their phenomenal rise in popularity. Indeed, they are now often considered to be an integral part of the home. Much of the upsurge of interest in their cultivation is due to the influence of the countries which experience long cold winters and, consequently, rely on indoor plants to provide colour and decoration. Equally important, as any enthusiast for these plants will confirm, is the interest provided by their remarkable diversity and the challenge they offer to the indoor gardener.

This highly informative, heavily illustrated book by a distinguished author is concerned with the cultivation of these plants. The coverage is wide, for house plants and succulents include an enormous range of fascinating material. The author has listed most of the genera of house plants suitable for permanent indoor decoration currently available in this country, and besides describing them – with a number code to indicate relative ease of culture – provides details of cultivation and propagation and discusses how best to group and display the plants.

Cacti and other succulent plants are touched on briefly in the first section of the book as house plants rather than a hobby subject, which is the basic theme of the second half of the book. This half is devoted to the collection and growing of succulents in both greenhouse and home conditions, and includes a descriptive list of over 70 genera. The small size of many kinds makes it possible to grow a large selection in a restricted space and this, together with the fascination and curiosity value of their varying shapes and often remarkable flowers, means that the growing of succulents can easily become a specialist interest and a most absorbing hobby.

Anthony Huxley

house plants cacti and succulents

HAMLYN
London · New York · Sydney · Toronto

contents

First Published 1972 by
The Hamlyn Publishing Group Limited
London · New York · Sydney · Toronto
Hamlyn House, Feltham, Middlesex, England
Second Impression 1973

Printed in Hong Kong by
Dai Nippon Printing Co., (International) Ltd.

what is a house plant?

The definition of a house plant which I have adopted in this book (with a few exceptions) is a plant which can remain as an almost permanent inhabitant of a room and which looks attractive all the time.

It is often a tropical or sub-tropical plant which is grown, in rooms, for its foliage alone, as greenhouse conditions are usually necessary to produce flowers on this type of plant. The flowering greenhouse plants so freely sold in pots will not continue to live happily in a room, nor can they normally be brought into flower in room conditions.

Many books on the subject include all sorts of exotic plants, such as hibiscus and orchids. In America and Scandinavia, where whole windows and sometimes entire rooms are filled with plants, conditions are often adjusted to resemble those of a greenhouse, and there such flowers can be grown, and indeed any of the varied selection of flowering greenhouse plants.

The average older house, however, is not hermetically sealed in winter, with air-conditioning and temperature thermostatically controlled. Its windows are often opened, and may let in the cold even when closed; it is draughty; it does not always have central heating; the air is dry, and the temperature is frequently high in the evenings and very low at night. These are not ideal conditions for house plants to flourish.

Now, there are some plants which will stand up to the worst of such conditions; but clearly the more we can adjust the environment to the ideal – constant adequate warmth, reasonably humid atmosphere and draughtlessness – the better the plants will like it and the greater the variety we can grow.

We must also remember that plants in pots must have a lot of attention. We cannot treat them as mere ornaments which only need dusting. They require watering, cleaning, occasional feeding and re-potting. Anyone who is not prepared to give his plants at least an hour's attention each week will inevitably fail with them. To those who will give some care, the plants will bring pleasure and interest as a living decoration.

In this half of the book my main object is to describe those plants which should thrive permanently in a living-room without recourse at any time to a greenhouse or garden, and to outline the care and cultivation necessary, with specific reference to the average home. I have attempted to include in it all the important genera which are commercially available at the present time, but, of course, new introductions are always being made. In passing, I will suggest the best means of keeping the flowering 'gift plants' in a reasonable state for as long as possible, and mention other classes of plant – annuals and succulents – which can be introduced into rooms.

general cultivation

Temperature and humidity

Many house plants will stand a considerable variation in temperature though they do need protection from frost, and, of course, it is best to avoid a high temperature by day and a very low one at night. But the air humidity must be adequate whatever the temperature; dry air is very bad for plants and causes discoloration, withering and dropping of the leaves. Now the amount of moisture which air can hold increases as the temperature rises; therefore, given only a limited amount of available moisture, air in a cool room is likely to be relatively more humid than that in a hot room.

If plants are to be grown in fairly warm conditions, especially if centrally heated, they must either be chosen for their dry-air resistance, or the local humidity must be improved. This can be done in several ways. Occasional misting of the foliage with clean water from a fine-nozzled syringe or spray bottle does a lot of good. The simplest means, however, is to stand the pots on a tray of pebbles or grit which is kept damp below pot level, or to use a trough-shaped container and plunge the pots in moist peat or sphagnum moss. Single pots can be stood on a block of wood surrounded by water in a saucer; it is often an advantage to use boiling water as the rising steam damps the leaves admirably. The water must not come up to the level of the bottom of the pot. With any of these methods water will evaporate steadily and provide air humidity around the leaves.

Ventilation

Stuffiness should be avoided, and fresh air supplied when the weather is not cold. But nothing kills a plant quicker than a draught.

Natural light

Most house plants prefer good indirect light, though sunlight rarely harms them. Spindly growth indicates lack of light. Plants tend to turn their stems and leaves towards light; turn them regularly to avoid uneven growth.

Artificial light

Electric light can be used to good effect in dark positions, to assist the flowering of difficult plants like African Violets, or to keep plants in indoor greenhouses growing properly. Fluorescent mercury-vapour tubes are recommended, particularly those suggested for plant cultivation which have a 'warm' light. Such tubes, which should be 9–12 in. apart, can be as little as 9 in. above African Violets, but for ordinary plants 18–24 in. is adequate. If the tubes are the sole or main source of light, they should be kept on for 12 to 16 hours a day.

It is possible to buy made-up units consisting of a tray for plant pots and a simple frame which supports a 2 ft. fluorescent tube above the plants.

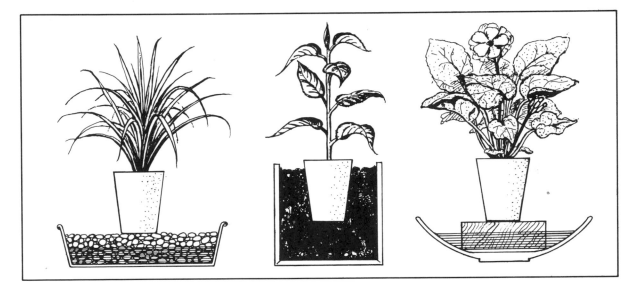

Ordinary incandescent bulbs give out less light and much more heat per watt than fluorescent tubes. For this reason they will scorch plants if too close, and are seldom of value to help indoor plants.

Watering

The aim when watering should be to prevent the soil from ever drying right out while avoiding sodden conditions which can be quite as bad, especially in winter, resulting in stagnant, airless soil in which the roots rot. When the soil starts to become dry – be guided by the look and feel of it; dry soil is hard to the touch and greyish-white in appearance – give a thorough watering. Never water in continual driblets, nor let plants stand in water-filled saucers. In summer, plants may need water two or three times a week, and an occasional soaking of the whole plant is beneficial; in winter, weekly or even fortnightly may be enough, depending on room temperature. A watering-can with a long, narrow spout will be found to be the most useful, since the water can be directed accurately into small pots and among foliage. It is advisable to use water at room temperature: some plants will drop their leaves or rot if chilled.

Watering presents difficulties when one goes on holiday. If no one can be found to do this, a useful tip is to soak the pot thoroughly and then put it in a polythene bag, either

5

(Below)
Aechmea fasciata is a striking house plant, with large strap-like, recurving leaves, marked with light and dark bands of grey, surrounding a central flower head of pink and blue

(Bottom)
Aeschynanthus grandiflorus makes a pleasing display, with bright flowers and shiny leaves

tying this round the stem of the plant at soil level or enclosing the whole plant within it. A pot so wrapped should keep damp for two or three weeks. An alternative is to use thin wicks or domestic tape leading into the pots from a vessel of water placed above them. The wicks should be soaked first to encourage the flow of water to the pots by capillarity. Put the plants in the coolest and shadiest place available – a larder is excellent. Many plants will tolerate standing in water in a sink for not more than two weeks, but let them drain thoroughly after this treatment.

Cleaning

Inevitably plants in a room become dusty, and in a town industrial grime may also accumulate on them. Apart from looking unpleasant and reducing the light reaching the leaves, this will clog the breathing pores of the leaves. Plants may be syringed or dipped in tepid soapy water, and then rinsed in clear water; a good place to do this is the bath. Those which cannot be moved should have their leaves gently sponged. Washing in this manner will also help to keep down insect pests. It is, however, important to ensure that water does not remain on leaves, especially hairy ones, or in the angle between leaf and stem, as rotting or scorching may follow.

Acclimatisation

It is best to buy plants in late spring and summer when conditions in the grower's greenhouse and your room are fairly similar. In winter the difference between these sets of conditions can be enormous and the plant receives a considerable check in its move. A summer-bought plant will also have the opportunity to acclimatise gradually to quite poor winter room conditions.

Re-potting and feeding

After a season or two, pots become filled with

roots (pot-bound). At this stage a shift into a slightly larger pot is desirable, and is best done in early summer. A good compost recipe is 2 parts of fibrous loam, 2 parts of rotted leaf-mould or peat and 1 part of coarse sand. Alternatively, John Innes Potting Compost No. 1 can be used, adding 1 or 2 parts of leaf-mould or peat to every 3 parts of compost. The soil-less composts based largely on peat, now freely available, are quite satisfactory for house plants but the nutrients in them are soon used up so that plants must be fed regularly after two or three months. This also applies to plants grown in the first mentioned compost recipe.

Newly bought or re-potted plants in soil-based composts will not need feeding, but those beginning to become pot-bound may be fed during the summer. Use a balanced fertiliser, preferably in weak solution, according to the maker's instructions, once or twice a month. Overfeeding results in weak growth and scorched foliage.

Both plastic and clay pots are equally suitable for house plants but remember that plants in plastic pots will need watering less often, while the clay pots must be well crocked to assist drainage.

Topdressing Plants which dislike being re-potted may have the soil partly replenished by topdressing. This consists of removing the top 1 or 2 in. of soil from the pot, taking care not to damage any roots, and replacing it with fresh compost containing fertilisers.

Cutting back

If plants grow too leggy, or if bushy growth is desired, many will benefit from being cut back periodically or from having the growing tip pinched out. Some rather difficult plants, like aphelandras and pileas, may lose most of their leaves during the winter. If so, cut them back to 2 inches above soil level in spring; new growth should sprout from the base.

(Below)
Aglaonema **Silver Queen is a compact plant which grows happily in rooms with central heating**
(Bottom)
The common name for *Anthurium scherzerianum* is Flamingo Flower; the spathes are as exotically coloured as the plumage of its namesake

7

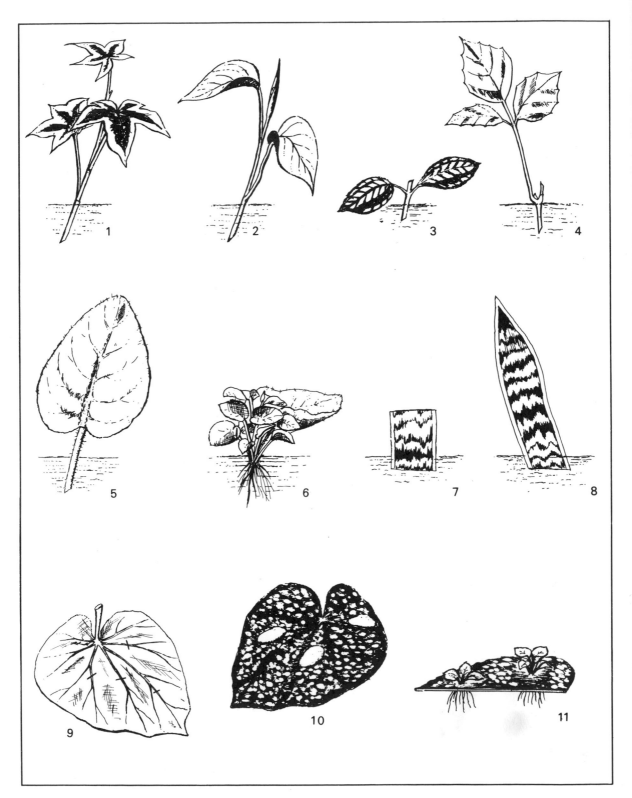

Propagation

Most indoor plants can be increased fairly readily from cuttings or offsets, often by division, and sometimes by layering. Raising from seed is normally too lengthy. The suitable method of increase for the individual plants is given in the List in Chapter Five.

Cuttings and offsets Cuttings are pieces of stem, occasionally separate leaves, or sometimes a leaf with a piece of stem attached. Types of cuttings are shown in the line drawing on page 8. A few will root in the open, or in water, but it is better to use a closed propagating case – a seed box supplied with glass sides bound with sticky tape and with a glass lid is quite suitable, or a more elaborate case may be made or bought. This must be kept out of direct sunlight.

The best time for rooting cuttings is in summer, unless bottom heat is available when rooting can start in spring. Sharp sand or vermiculite, or a mixture of these with peat, is used as a rooting medium. It should be kept fairly damp. If only one or two cuttings are wanted, a jam-jar or polythene bag over a pot can replace the case. Cuttings of woody plants will root quicker if hormone rooting powders are used.

As soon as the cutting has rooted, pot it up in an individual pot of light, sandy soil, and acclimatise it carefully to the room conditions.

Offsets are small growths produced round certain plants (i.e. bromeliads, clivias), and they can be grown on like cuttings. They can often be taken with some roots, when they should be treated like newly rooted cuttings, and potted into small pots.

Division Many plants can be increased by division of clumps; this should be done with

(Left)
1 and 2: fatshedera and philodendron stem cuttings taken from ends of shoots; 3 and 4: pilea and rhoicissus cuttings taken from sections of stems bearing leaves; 5 and 6: saintpaulia leaf cutting, plant formed where leaf stem enters the soil; 7 and 8: rooting sections of sansevieria leaves; 9–11: begonia, gloxinia and other thick-veined leaves cut on veins on underside and laid flat on sand with pebble to keep them in place

(Below)
Air layering. 12: make 1-in. slit up stem or, 13: cut out ½-in. ring of bark; 14 and 15: dust with hormone rooting powder, bind moist sphagnum moss around stem, surround with polythene and tie top and bottom; 16: when roots appear cut stem below these and pot up

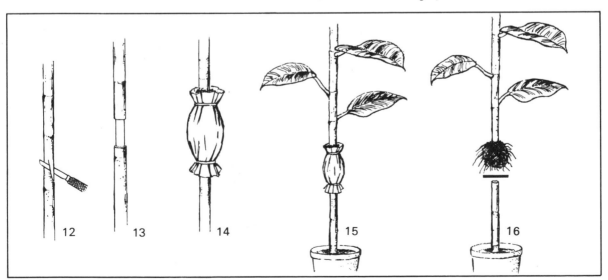

care so as not to damage too many roots. Water carefully for a time after dividing, which is best done in late spring.

Layering This consists of bending a branch into a pot of soil, where it is firmly pegged, preferably cutting into the lower surface of the piece underground to provide a 'tongue', as with carnations. Hormone rooting powders can be dusted into the cut with advantage. When roots have been formed, the layer can be cut off from the parent.

Air layering Also known as Chinese layering, this is ideal for plants such as *Ficus*, *Fatshedera* and *Dracaena* which become leggy due to the lower leaves falling. Though the tops of these can be used as cuttings, a good deal of heat is needed for success. To make an air layer, either make a slit about 1 in. long into the stem, from below upwards, and push a sliver of wood into it to hold it open, or cut out a ring of bark about $\frac{1}{2}$ in. wide, in each case at the point where roots are wanted. (See line drawing on page 9.) Dust the cut with a hormone rooting powder if available. Next, bind a handful of moist sphagnum moss or peat around the cut with a few turns of thread, and then surround this with polythene sheet (or a polythene bag cut open), overlapping it well and tying firmly top and bottom. A few weeks after roots show through the moss the stem may be cut below the moss ball and the new plant can be carefully potted up. Make sure plenty of roots have formed before cutting the stem: usually at least eight weeks is necessary for this. The old stem will sprout again, usually near the point of cut, or it may be reduced further to ensure more attractive new growth nearer the base of the old plant.

For air layering it is best to use only the top of the plant, say the upper 12–24 in., where the stem is the least woody.

(Below)
This saintpaulia has become pot bound and is being potted on to a size-larger pot. The soil ball is loosened by banging the rim of the pot. The pot is held in one hand and the plant can then be freed gently

(Bottom)
Crocks and a little fresh soil are placed at the bottom of the new pot. The plant is held in position just below rim level and fresh soil dribbled down the sides. Firm gently

(Below)
When leaves are dirty they can be washed in a bucket or bath of water. Wrap a cloth round the base of the stem to prevent the plant coming away from the pot

(Bottom)
Dirt can be removed from large-surfaced leaves by gently sponging with tepid water

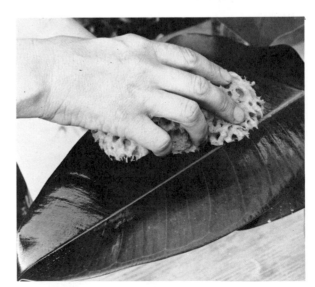

plant health

Apart from a few insect pests and possibly mildew, ill health in house plants is almost always due to external conditions or cultivation faults. It is seldom possible to tell what is wrong with the plant merely by looking at it; one has to consider the conditions and previous treatment. Below is given a list of possible symptoms and their alternative causes. Many of these symptoms may also show up on plants not properly acclimatised and, therefore, are most frequently seen in winter. Details of insect pests are given later, together with general remedies.

SYMPTOMS

Weak, spindly growth Lack of light; excess winter heat.

A check or reduction in growth: production of small leaves A sudden change in conditions; overwatering; overfeeding; often exhaustion of soil or excessive dryness at roots.

Dry spots, patches or margins on leaves Overwatering; overfeeding; draughts; sun scorch; water on leaves in strong sun; gas fumes; hot dry air; thrips or scale insects.

Leaves yellowing (followed eventually by leaf fall) Leaves at base of stems will naturally yellow and fall occasionally, but when several or all do it something is clearly amiss. Overwatering; overfeeding; exhaustion of soil; dryness at roots; draughts; excessive cold; gas fumes; hot, dry air; red spider.

Leaves falling suddenly A sudden change in conditions; draughts; watering with cold water; gas fumes; lack of light in winter; excessive sun suddenly in spring.

Leaves distorted or blistered, often yellowing Aphids.

Small raised waxy mounds Scale insects.

White mealy insects Mealy bugs.

General yellowing and poor appearance (in succulents, especially cacti) Exhaustion of soil; root mealy bug.

Complete collapse Frost; excessive cold; excessive sun, particularly on pot; gas fumes; complete drying out of soil.

Wilting Dryness at roots; excessive sun; sometimes waterlogged soil.

Rotting of leaves or stems Fungus attack due to damage or bad conditions; very rarely direct infection.

Whitish powdering on leaves Mildew, usually on overcrowded plants; overwatering; excessive humidity.

Bud and flower drop Overwatering, dryness at roots; air too dry; scorching sun; fluctuating temperatures; draughts; moving plants from one place to another.

INSECT PESTS

Aphids (green or black fly) These common pests suck the sap, causing leaves to twist up, turn yellow and eventually fall, and may also damage growing tips. Young aphids are

(Left)
Begonia rex is an excellent foliage plant with many handsome varieties
(Right)
The fibrous-rooting ***Begonia semperflorens*** is an easily cared for house plant
(Below right)
Begonia masoniana, one of the finest foliage begonias, is admirably suited to mixed plantings
(Bottom right)
Begonia lucerna is a highly decorative plant with a long flowering period

hardly visible, being pale and less than 1 mm. long. *Control:* small colonies may be wiped out by hand, or spray with an insecticide such as malathion or dimethoate. (Do not use malathion on crassulas or ferns.)

Mealy bug A kind of aphid, broad, white, woolly and about $\frac{1}{8}$ in. long. *Control:* pick off individuals with a paint brush soaked in methylated spirit or malathion solution, or spray with malathion.

Red spiders Tiny reddish mites, which suck sap and multiply rapidly; encouraged by hot, dry air. Any mottling or yellowing of leaves should be regarded with suspicion and the undersides examined. While the mites are just visible to the practised eye, a lens is desirable to confirm the diagnosis. When a large colony is present, a white webbing is produced. *Control:* where possible, fairly strong syringing with water on leaf undersides. Spray plant with derris, malathion or dimethoate.

Root mealy bug Similar to mealy bug, infesting roots (mainly on succulents) where it makes a white woolly mass. *Control:* shake off soil, wash roots, remove pests with a paint brush dipped in methylated spirit, or water soil with liquid malathion.

Scale insects A kind of aphid which settles down in one place, forming a tiny waxy mound, later followed by yellowing around the mound as the insect sucks the sap.

Control : wipe off with a soft cloth or paint brush soaked in warm soapy water or methylated spirit; spray badly infected plants with malathion or dimethoate.

Thrips Small, thin insects, $\frac{1}{8}$ in. long, which jump when disturbed and cause small brown or white marks on leaves and flowers. *Control* : spray with malathion or derris.

General After dealing with an insect attack on one plant, keep an eye on it for several weeks, as very young insects or eggs may not be wiped out; also examine neighbouring plants carefully. If a bad attack occurs a general spraying should be carried out when the plants are being cleaned. It is important that all chemicals should be used strictly according to manufacturer's instructions. Many insecticides have a harmful effect on fish and other livestock and to safeguard pets it is a good idea to treat plants in a sheltered position out of doors. Dimethoate is a systemic insecticide, which means that it passes into the plant's sap and provides protection for several weeks.

Minute grubs which turn into very small flies may appear in the pot soil. They are almost always quite harmless but can be eradicated by watering with malathion.

REMEDIES

The action to take for the majority of the complaints listed above is obvious: the most important thing being to observe the first signs of trouble, deduce the cause and act on this immediately. Many of these symptoms can be detected when the plants are given their regular cleaning, and some – including most insect attacks – will hardly occur if regular cleaning is given.

The remedy may not always be so easy. Mildew may be cleaned off, or a fungicide such as thiram or colloidal copper be applied. Rotting is, as stated, usually a secondary symptom. All rotten parts should be removed

at once. If the base of the stem is involved, cut off the healthy top and treat this, if possible, as a cutting. The same advice applies when a plant has lost most of its basal leaves. When a plant is suffering from drought, the pot should be stood in water for some hours. A plant which has been thoroughly overwatered should be allowed to dry out completely, but severe damage has often been done before the cause of the symptoms has been realised. A frost-damaged plant may be rescued by gradually thawing it out in a dark, cool place.

BASIC RULES

If the following points are watched, little should go wrong with the plants, assuming that they have been chosen to suit the existing conditions.

1. Do not waterlog the soil or allow the pot to stand in water too long.
2. Make sure the drainage is adequate and has not become clogged.
3. Do not use very cold water.
4. Do not let the soil dry right out.
5. Water sparingly in winter (in general).
6. Do not water by the calendar – check by feeling the soil.
7. Do not feed too often, with too much or too strong a solution.
8. Feed well-established plants only.
9. Clean plants regularly.
10. Re-pot plants as required; but do not keep looking at the roots.
11. Keep out draughts.
12. Make sure any gas appliance is not leaking.
13. Try to keep the air round the plants moist.
14. Avoid sun scorch and keep sun off the plant and pot.
15. Avoid direct hot air from any radiators reaching plants.
16. Avoid widely fluctuating temperatures and stuffy air.
17. Avoid shutting plants between curtain and window on cold nights.

where to grow house plants

Individual plants

Clay pots are admirable for growing plants in, but they cannot be said to be beautiful. The first thing to do is to conceal the pots, and a variety of 'pothiders' is available of cane, wicker, raffia, split wood, metal, etc. These will serve for a few plants, which can be stood here and there in the room, each in its own saucer. Too many individual plants, however, will make a lot of work and produce a restless, untidy atmosphere. When this happens, it is best to group the plants together in troughs, baskets or other containers, of which a very large range can be bought.

Climbers

Individual climbing plants can be accommodated on their own trellis-work, made from cane or wicker pushed into the soil of the pot, and tied at the junctions. Many patterns will suggest themselves including 'free' arrangements made of thick wicker steamed, bent to shape, and cooled in that position. See line drawing on page 20.

Climbers with aerial roots can be grown on a branch or stick to which sphagnum moss is thickly bound with copper wire. The roots enter the damp moss and the plant grows luxuriantly in a natural way. Such plants include *Ficus pumila*, *Hedera* (ivies), *Hoya*, *Philodendron*, *Scindapsus* and *Syngonium*.

Plants on walls Where a wall space is available climbers can be trained on it effectively. An almost invisible support is provided by thin copper wire or strong thread stretched from skirting board to picture rail, but if a more formal effect is wanted, various materials can be used, such as expanded metal, wood trellis or criss-crossed bamboos.

Troughs and jardinières

For most plants and most rooms, however, a trough-shaped container is a particularly useful one. For one thing, a trough with solid or mesh sides can be filled with damp peat or moss into which the pots are plunged, as already described, to improve air humidity. Such long narrow containers can also be easily positioned – along the window is often ideal both for the plants and to fit with the furniture, or they can be placed at right angles to the window at one side. A very decorative effect is obtained by 'framing' the window with climbing plants, which can meet at the top, with a trough at or below sill level.

A wheeled trolley, with the plants on a tray, can be useful in a small room. By day it can be kept near the window, by night moved into the room. This is also an admirable way for an invalid to have and tend a selection of plants.

Plant associations

The grouping of plants will depend upon

continue on page 21

(Left)
Clivia miniata has striking red or orange flowers which it should produce regularly if carefully treated

(Below)
The beautiful translucent leaves of *Calathea makoyana* make it a spectacular plant, especially suitable for bottle gardens

(Right)
This fine example of *Cissus antarctica* shows its climbing characteristic to advantage. It does not like hot, dry conditions

**Climbing plants need some support and this can
be provided by tying wicker canes together.
Thick wicker can also be steamed and curved**

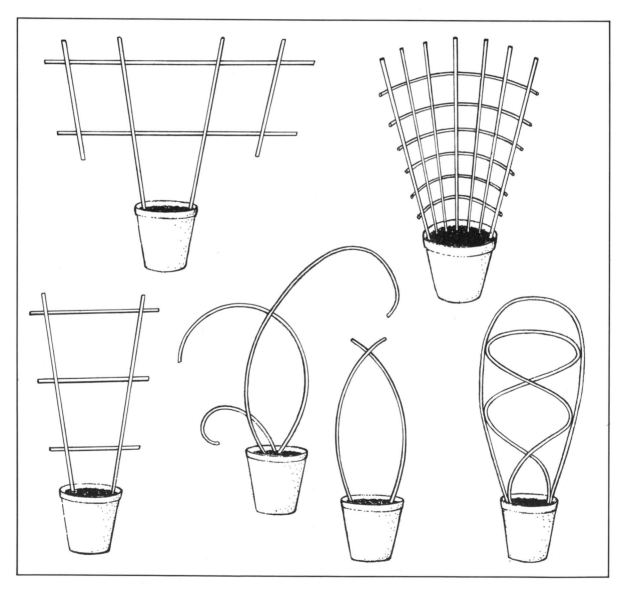

personal taste. There are all shapes and sizes to choose from, including a few which may be best placed quite alone. Each plant should be positioned to set off its neighbours; trailing plants will break the outlines of the container and conceal pots; low bushy plants will fit in at the base of a tall-stemmed one; rosette plants will give solidity; climbers will give background; and so on.

Leaf colour is as important as shape, and it will be found that there is great variation even in the basic green; some leaves are grey or bluish, a few red or brown, while very many plants are striped, banded or mottled in various ways – variegation is the generic term – in white, cream, yellow, silver and red. Apparent fading of variegation is usually due to excessive shade. If non-variegated shoots appear these should be pinched out or they may in time supersede the variegated ones.

Ornamental bowls

There is an increasing tendency to group plants closely together in bowls or other containers, in effect creating an artistic arrangement as one does with cut flowers. The plants can either be left in their pots, which are concealed beneath moss or peat, or can be tipped out and 'planted', though without disturbing the roots, in peat. Undrained containers are quite satisfactory as long as watering is cautious and water does not collect in them, but such arrangements are basically temporary, and the plants should be given a periodic respite in pots. Very attractive combinations can be achieved, and flowering plants can be included for short spells.

Glass indoors

Various kinds of indoor greenhouse have been marketed, some simply a metal-framed box, others with a peaked roof like a real greenhouse and with a solid waterproof base. It is easy enough for a handyman to construct such a

case; ideally it has sliding glass sides and top. These indoor greenhouses are derived from the Victorian Wardian Case, a glass structure which remained virtually sealed, and their merit is, of course, the maintenance of the high humidity needed by plants such as marantas which otherwise succeed only in bottle gardens (see below). Heating may be installed, best by means of a tubular electric heater or a soil-warming cable, or by placing the greenhouse over a radiator. Such greenhouses must be kept in good light, or provided with mercury-vapour light tubes (see page 4), or the plants will become spindly.

Bottle gardens

An amusing room decoration which has become very popular is the bottle garden. Any large bottle can be used, but an acid or distilled water carboy is ideal: bottles with an opening less than $1\frac{1}{2}$ in. across are difficult to plant. After thoroughly cleaning the glass a 1 in. layer of crocks should be put in. This is followed by soil 5–6 in. deep, using either 2 parts John Innes Potting Compost No. 1 with 1 part extra peat, or a mixture of 1 part loam, 2 parts peat and 1 part coarse sand. It is best delivered through a funnel of stout paper to avoid dirtying the glass. It should be slightly moist but *not* wet. Firm the soil as filling proceeds with a cotton reel fixed on the end of a cane. Next arrange the plants as they are to be planted, so that you can work from outside to centre, thus avoiding dropping soil on the plants. Make a hole to receive the plant with a pointed piece of lath – the hole must be large enough to start with – and then, removing enough soil from the rootball to allow it through the opening, push the plant in, let it drop and manipulate it into place with lath and a cane. Cover the roots up, and firm with the cotton reel. It is not as difficult as it sounds: a little practice and a lot of patience will produce an object as intriguing as a ship

(Left)
The codiaeums provide an astonishing range of leaf colour and form

(Below left)
The bold markings of dieffenbachia are shown to advantage when it is used as a specimen plant

(Bottom left)
This is *Cordyline terminalis* Red Edge; others have yellow, silver and purple variegation

(Right)
Cryptanthus bromelioides tricolor and *C. zonatus* are both excellent plants for a bottle garden

in a bottle. A little water every month or two in the summer is all the bottle requires, and it need not be sealed as condensation then forms on the glass. Dead leaves are twisted or broken off by pressure from a cane, and pulled out on a pointed stick or hooked wire, or a razor blade may be wired to a cane for necessary surgery – which needs considerable care.

Similar gardens can be made in goldfish bowls, large brandy glasses or wide-necked storage jars.

A normal-sized carboy will hold seven to nine plants, which should be obtained in the smallest possible pots. The following are recommended:

Calatheas; *Cocos weddeliana* or *Neanthe elegans* (dwarf palms); cryptanthuses; *Ficus radicans variegata;* fittonias; *Helxine soleirolii* (will carpet the soil); marantas; peperomias; pileas; selaginellas; small ferns such as *Asplenium nidus, Pellaea rotundifolia* and *Pteris* species.

Varieties of *Cordyline terminalis, Dieffenbachia picta, Dracaena fragrans, D. deremensis* and *D. sanderiana* can be used if a larger plant is wanted.

Flowering plants are not recommended for bottle gardening, as they are seldom satisfactory for long, but they can be used in goldfish bowls where attention can be given easily. Avoid vigorous plants like tradescantias and chlorophytums which grow much too fast.

(Below, left and right)
When planting a bottle garden, put in the plants round the edge first; dig a good-sized hole for each, push the soil all round the plant and finally make it really firm

(Bottom)
Bottle gardens can be made in a wide range of containers, including large carboys, cider and wine flagons, sweet jars and goldfish bowls

An interesting contrast in house plant forms in a bowl arrangement. The plants are *Philodendron bipinnatifidum, Cissus antarctica,* codiaeum, peperomias, *Saxifraga stolonifera* and *Maranta leuconeura kerchoveana*

(Below)
Plants will benefit from the equable temperature which this growing case provides. Strip lights inside the case attractively illuminate the plants

(Bottom)
Decorative pot covers and containers add gaiety to plant display. A wide selection is now available in a variety of materials including pottery, clay, plastic and polystyrene. Miniature cultivating tools are also available

house plants to grow

In the Alphabetical List which follows, I have given brief descriptions and cultivation details of over eighty genera of permanent house plants you might choose to grow.

There are, of course, many other plants which can be grown in rooms. A number of hardy plants, from trees to alpines, will grow in cool, sunny windows. At the other end of the scale, anyone who can provide a greenhouse atmosphere by one means or another can grow any greenhouse plant, depending upon the heat available. In this last category come a variety of genera occasionally offered, including *Alocasia, Bertolonia, Bougainvillea, Crossandra, Dipladenia, Episcia, Eranthemum, Gardenia, Hoffmania, Ixora, Miconia, Piper, Sanchezia* and *Sonerila*.

Succulents, including cacti, are excellent in a sunny window. Their treatment in rooms is outlined on page 60, and they are dealt with in detail on pages 66 to 128. Another large group are the Bromeliads (page 36), which include many good house plants. More or less temporary 'gift plants' are described under *Florists' Plants* (page 47), and the few annuals which can be grown indoors under *Annuals* (page 28). Limitations of length have forced me to omit all bulbous plants.

(Left)
The shiny leaf textures of the rubber plant, codiaeum and variegated ivy complement each other in this homely setting

Ease of cultivation

The figure 1, 2, 3 or 4 placed after the name of each plant is a rough indication of its ease of cultivation. Plants marked 1 are easy to grow in almost any conditions; 2 indicates plants which it should be possible to grow in average conditions with a little experience and care. Plants marked 3 are rather difficult, needing something better than the 'average' room and a good deal of care. Those classed under 4 have become popular in countries where central heating and air-conditioning are commonly available, and are usually more suitable for growing in indoor greenhouses than in the normal open room. This classification is also a very rough guide to the degree of heat needed, which, in many rooms, is still often the deciding factor. A cold room is, of course, one that is not heated at all. 'Cool' conditions mean a minimum of 4–7°C. (40–45°F.) and a maximum of 13°C. (55°F.). When 'some heat' is noted, this means between 10–18°C. (50–65°F.). A few plants described need a minimum of 16°C. (60°F.).

The abbreviation P. stands for Propagation. Do not forget that, unless otherwise stated, winter watering and the atmospheric conditions needed for each plant are as described in Chapter Two.

Some of these plants have English names, and these have been given and cross-referenced where they are in reasonably common use. They all have Latin names; as in every form of gardening, one simply has to get used to them. They are really more use than English names!

DESCRIPTIVE LIST

Acorus (1) *A. gramineus variegatus* is a fleshy-rooted plant like a miniature flag iris, its fan of leaves cream-striped longwise. It makes a useful contrast in a bottle garden. It should be kept very moist and rather cool. P., division.

Adiantum (3) The maidenhair ferns are old favourites, with elegant small leaflets on wiry black stems. They are, however, difficult house plants, detesting sun, gas, tobacco smoke, sooty atmosphere, dry air and draughts. Few rooms can provide conditions in which they will live long, though they thrive in an indoor greenhouse. *A. capillus-veneris* (up to 12 in. high) and its many varieties, *A. venustum* (to 12 in.) and *A. pedatum* (to 24 in.), are nearly hardy and need cool, moist conditions; *A. cuneatum* (9 in.) needs some heat. General cultivation, see *Ferns*.

Aechmea (2) A large genus of attractive bromeliads, making tall, sculptural 'leaf-vase' rosettes. Only a few are in commerce. *A. fulgens* has 16-in. very recurved, wavy green leaves, purple beneath. *A. fasciata* (also known as *Billbergia rhodocyanea*) has broad, white-banded, grey-green leaves up to 2 ft. long. Cultivation, see *Bromeliads*.

Aeschynanthus (4) Plants with colourful flowers like those of *Columnea* but in clusters. Hothouse subjects which may survive flowerless in a room but really need the humidity of an indoor greenhouse. Partly synonymous with *Trichosporum*. Cultivation the same as for *Columnea*.

African Violet See *Saintpaulia*.

Aglaonema (2) A number of species, sometimes called Chinese Evergreens, with oval or more elongated leaves which are often attrac-tively marbled, or more rarely symmetrically patterned. Good plants especially for central heating, tolerating shade but never gas fumes. Use a compost with extra peat. P., division, or cuttings in heat.

Aluminium Plant See *Pilea*.

Ampelopsis (2) This genus of Virginia Creepers gives us one house plant, *A. heterophylla* (syn. *brevipedunculata elegans*), in which the stems are pink and the usually 3-lobed leaves pink, white and cream. Their thin texture makes them resent dry, stuffy air, but in a cool or cold place it makes a striking climber – except that it naturally loses its leaves in winter. P., cuttings.

Ananas (2) The common pineapple, *A. comosus*, is a bromeliad, and makes an attractive plant of some size, with its long-toothed leaves – up to 5 ft. long in nature – especially in the variegated and coloured-leaved forms. It is possible to obtain a plant by cutting off the top of a fresh pineapple fruit, removing all the flesh and placing it in sand kept moist in some heat (ideally, 21–27°C. [70–80 °F.]), when it may root. Cultivation, see *Bromeliads*.

Annuals A number of climbing plants, either annual or normally treated as such, have proved suitable for rooms, providing quick growth and attractive flowers in summer following spring sowing.

Convolvulus major, Ipomoea tricolor (rubro-caerulea), Thunbergia alata, Tropaeolum majus and *T. peregrinum* will flower in a cool room; *Cobaea scandens, Maurandya barclaiana* and *Rhodochiton volubile* need some heat (at least 10°C. [50°F.]) and humidity, especially to start with. *Passiflora caerulea* may also be grown from seed, mainly for its foliage. *Eucalyptus globulus* is a quick-growing tree which makes several feet of growth in one season, and is treated like the climbers.

Seeds of all these may be sown in small pots between February and April, the date depending upon the degree of heat and the amount of air moisture available. If no special facilities can be provided for germination and the first weeks of growth, such as a propagating case, it is best to wait till early April or, alternatively, to buy greenhouse-grown seedlings in April, May or June. It is essential to maintain steady growth, not allowing the plants to be checked by cold, draughts or becoming pot-bound; they must be potted on until they are in 4-in. or 5-in. pots at least. Two or three plants may be placed in a large pot to make dense growth. Lack of light at any stage will make them grow spindly, and they may not make up for this.

Once growing steadily, and especially when flower buds begin to form, regular feeding will benefit the plants greatly – little, weak and often being the rule. The climbers must, of course, have stakes or strings on which to climb, or a simple cane trellis may be made by pushing two canes into the pot to form a diverging angle, with cross-pieces tied on at spaced intervals.

Most garden annuals are not suitable for growing from seed indoors in this way.

Anthurium (3) Relatives of the arum lily, some grown for their flowers and some for their leaves, all rather difficult, needing constant moist heat (16°C. [60°F.] minimum), partial shade and plenty of water. Central heating suits them, as long as damp moss or gravel is placed to evaporate moisture and maintain humidity around them (see page 4). *A. andreanum* with long, heart-shaped leaves and *A. scherzerianum*, with white-veined, ribbon-like leaves, are smallish plants, the leaves 6–8 in. long, grown for their long-lasting flowers, which are produced most of the year. The latter, the Flamingo Flower, is easier in rooms. There are many hybrids, with orange, scarlet, pink or white blooms, looking like distorted arum lilies. A suitable compost contains peat, loam, sphagnum moss and sand. P., division, seed, in hot, moist conditions. When re-potting, take great care of the roots.

Aphelandra (3) Several species are grown in warm greenhouses; one, *A. squarrosa louisae,* has become popular as a house plant. The dark green 6–9 in. leaves are boldly marked with white along the veins, and in spring a cockade of bright yellow bracts is produced at the top. Despite its greenhouse origin, it does fairly well in a warm room; the temperature must not vary very much, and draughts and stuffy air must be avoided. Plenty of water should be given at all times. If many leaves drop in winter, cut hard back in spring. P., cuttings of sideshoots in heat.

Aralia See *Dizygotheca* and *Fatsia*.

Araucaria (1) *A. excelsa,* the Norfolk Island Pine, is a conifer with bright green, horizontal branches, looking like an artificial Christmas tree. It is nearly hardy, and only needs to be kept reasonably damp in a fairly moist, draught-free atmosphere. It will stand much shade and needs compost with extra peat. P., seed, cuttings, in heat.

Asparagus (1) The so-called asparagus ferns are really relatives of the lily. *A. plumosus* is the one with very fine, feathery foliage; *A. sprengeri* has 1-in. needle-like leaves; *A. asparagoides* or *A. medeoloides* (the Smilax of florists) has 1-in. oval leaves; while the very vigorous *A. falcatus* has 3-in. sickle-shaped leaves. All are long-stemmed climbers or can be used as trailers. *A. plumosus nanus* and *A. p. compactus* are small-growing varieties that need no support. They are easy plants, tolerating shade, which need frequent feeding and plenty of water, especially *A. sprengeri.* They sometimes produce tiny flowers followed by berries. P., seed, cuttings, in heat.

Aspidistra (1) The old Cast Iron Plant, indeed a relic of the Victorians, *A. lurida (elatior)* will stand deep shade and almost any neglect. It dislikes sunlight. In a large decorative scheme there may be a place for its massive 12–20-in. dark green leaves. There is a scarce, boldly white-striped form which is

more attractive. Keep fairly warm in winter. The weird soil-level flowers, occasionally borne, are pollinated by snails. P., division.

Asplenium (1, 2) A large genus of ferns, many easy in cool rooms, especially *A. bulbiferum* (1), with finely divided 1–2-ft. fronds on which young plants are produced, and *A. praemorsum* (1), with rather stiff 6–18-in. fronds. *A. nidus* (2), the Bird's Nest Fern, is very attractive, with undivided fronds from 6–24 in. long, tapering at both ends, of apple green with blackish midrib. It needs light and some warmth, and must be kept from draughts, or the leaves go brown. Good in bottle gardens. Cultivation, see *Ferns*.

Astilbe *(Spiraea)* See *Florists' Plants*.

Azalea indica (3) This beautiful florists' plant, freely sold in autumn and winter, with single or double flowers in pink, red or white, is one of the more difficult of temporary plants. It is forced in heat and humidity, and has a very compact rootball, usually potted in pure peat. This must be kept moist, for it dries out very easily; if this happens, the leaves and flowers will drop. The plant needs to be kept in a steady medium temperature, out of draughts, should be given a fine spray-over with water when possible, and does best when stood above water or damp peat (see page 4). Keep out of sunlight. When flowering is over, it can be placed in a cooler room but must still be treated with great care. Once the danger of frost is past, the plant should, if possible, be re-potted in compost with additional peat and stood outside, preferably burying the pot in soil. Regular watering, feeding and syringing during summer are necessary. In autumn it must be brought indoors before frost is likely, and may be persuaded to flower again in a room. P., summer cuttings. See also *Florists' Plants*.

Baby's Tears See *Helxine soleirolii*.

Begonia (2, 3) This immense genus supplies us with a number of house plants, moderately

(Left)
A collection of ferns – all easy to grow and ideal for a cold room – with helxine in front

(Below)
The spectacular epiphyllums will produce their vivid flowers in a warm room, but they need a peaty compost and good humidity

(Bottom)
An excellent group planting of *Ficus elastica tricolor, Ficus benjamina* and *Poinsettia* Paul Mikkelsen. With care and attention the poinsettia will last for several months

or fairly difficult to keep permanently; some give a long season of bloom, and most have decorative leaves, which are characteristically lop-sided. In general, they all need constant temperatures of at least 13°C. (55°F.) in winter, fairly high air humidity, clean air and absence of draughts. They like peaty compost with good drainage (soil-less composts are excellent), appreciate feeding, plenty of water, overhead spraying and good light without excess of sun. If they can be established, some make very effective specimens indoors.

For our purpose the begonias are best divided as follows. There is not space to mention here the large-flowered, tuberous-rooted begonias, which have a dormant period.

Foliage Begonias These are virtually stemless and are grown for their large, strikingly-marked foliage up to 12 in. long, in various shades of green, grey, silver, red, purple, etc. They need at least 13°C. (55°F.) and high humidity. They are greedy feeders. *Begonia rex* is the typical species but there are many others and innumerable hybrids. One of the most striking is Iron Cross *(B. masoniana)* with a brown pattern on bristly leaves; *B. boweri* is a small plant with black-edged leaves. P., leaf cuttings in heat.

Stem Begonias The least difficult house begonias come into this class. The following can be recommended: *B. corolicta, B. feastii, B. fuchsioides, B. glaucophylla, B. haageana, B. heracleifolia, B. ingrami, B. maculata, B. nitida, B. richardsiana.* There are also innumerable hybrids of which Beatrice Haddrell, Chantilly Lace and Cleopatra are extremely popular. Many of these species and hybrids will grow several feet tall, and may be cut back occasionally to keep them bushy. P., cuttings in some heat.

Semi-tuberous Begonias Orange-flowered *B. sutherlandii* and pink *B. weltoniensis* are small bushy plants which grow from tubers and die right down in the winter, when the pots should be stored virtually dry. Start watering again when new growth is seen.

Bedding Begonias These are dwarf fibrous-rooted varieties, very free flowering, derived from *B. semperflorens*. Though mainly used for summer bedding, they are quite perennial. They should be trimmed back now and then. P., cuttings, seed, in heat.

Gloire de Lorraine Begonias These winter-flowering hybrids (sometimes known as *B. cheimantha* or *B. hiemalis*) are hard to keep, though they may be used as temporary flowering plants and, if bought early enough and kept fairly cool, may survive the winter. P., leaf cuttings in heat.

Beloperone guttata (2) A shrubby plant, 2 or 3 ft. high, with arching spikes of smallish flowers partly concealed by large overlapping bracts in pink and brown, whose shape and colour give it the name Shrimp Plant; the flowers are carried more or less continuously in warm, moist air. It needs good drainage, and likes sun and some warmth, and frequent feeding. Water freely, but keep almost dry in winter. It tends to become leggy, so cut back in spring and root new plants periodically; non-flowering shoots do so readily.

Billbergia (1, 2) *B. nutans* (1) is the commonest of the cultivated bromeliads; it is almost hardy and will produce flowers in a warm room, which most of the tribe will not. It has an upright, recurving rosette of 1 ft.-long, narrow, spiny, dark green leaves, and the $1\frac{1}{2}$-in. tubular flowers, produced on long stems, are pink, yellow, green and blue. It should be pot-bound to flower. There are many more attractive species, but few are available. *B. windii* (1) is a hybrid of *B. nutans*, not unlike it, with larger flowers and leaves. *B. zebrina* (2) forms an 18-in. tubular rosette striped with grey. *B. rhodocyanea* (2) is *Aechmea fasciata*. Cultivation, see *Bromeliads*.

Bird's Nest Fern See *Asplenium nidus*.

continued on page 36

(Below)
Asparagus plumosus is an easy plant to grow and will tolerate shade, so is ideal for a badly lit room

(Bottom)
Asplenium nidus has attractive apple-green fronds which can grow to 24 in. It is a good plant for a bottle garden

(Left)
A fine example of *Fittonia verschaffeltii* with purple-veined leaves and showy bracts. It flourishes in a bottle garden

(Below)
The plants shown on this page are all easily obtainable from the florist. Fuchsias are popular with those who like flowering house plants

(Bottom)
There is a wide range of colouring in coleus, and with care they will live for some time

(Below)
The vivid trumpets of the gloxinia make it a welcome though temporary guest in any house

(Bottom)
Cyclamens will flower profusely from late autumn to early spring with proper care. *Cyclamen persicum* is the parent of these very decorative indoor varieties

(Below)
The tolerant chlorophytum is a popular house and office plant. This mature specimen has produced plantlets, each of which can be rooted individually

Bow-string Hemp See *Sansevieria trifasciata laurentii*.

Bromeliads (2) A large family *(Bromeliaceae)* of plants from tropical America, many of which are ideal room plants, usually very decorative and making large sculptural specimens. Despite their jungle origins, they are tolerant of quite difficult conditions and will stand much neglect. They are rosette plants, with leaves varying from ¼–4 in. across and up to many feet long, though, of course, those sold for rooms are not so large. The leaves are stiff, hard, usually spiny, and have a great variety of colourings, including bright red, brown, silver and grey, and are often beautifully mottled. The flowers are all extraordinary, both in shape and colour; much of the colour comes from bracts surrounding the flowers, which last a very long time. Rosettes which have flowered do not do so again and may die, but in any case it is difficult to flower most of the genera without a hot, humid greenhouse.

Most of them are epiphytic, living on trees, etc., but without being in any way parasitic, and are known in America as air pines, but some are terrestrial. A few of the epiphytes have leaves so closely packed together that they form a watertight 'vase' in the centre, and have special cells for absorbing this water. Some need little else besides water to survive.

A suitable compost for most bromeliads consists of 2 parts sphagnum moss, peat and/or leafmould, 1 part fibrous loam and 1 part coarse sand, with a few small pieces of charcoal, or equal parts fibrous loam and leafmould can be used. All need good drainage.

These plants must never be overwatered, especially in winter. Those with leaf-vases should have them filled, preferably with rainwater, but they still need light watering of the soil. They prefer a moist equable atmosphere and temperatures over 16 °C. (60 °F.), but will stand dry and colder air. Most types prefer daylight but can survive in shady conditions.

In general, propagation is from well-formed offsets, best rooted in heat; or from seed, a slow process.

The nomenclature of these plants, particularly in the trade, is somewhat confused; however, any bromeliad of reasonable size is worth acquiring. Descriptions of the following genera, species of which are in commerce, are given in the list: *Aechmea, Ananas, Billbergia, Cryptanthus, Guzmania, Neoregelia, Nidularium, Tillandsia* and *Vriesia*.

Busy Lizzie See *Impatiens*.

Cacti See *Succulents*.

Calathea (3) Attractive low-growing plants very similar to *Maranta* (page 50): in fact species and varieties are apt to be labelled indiscriminately under one name or the other. There are numerous species but only a few are available. Of these *C. makoyana*, the Peacock Plant, is the most spectacular, with curious red ellipses and lines on the pale green, translucent leaves. *C. oppenheimiana* (sometimes classed as a *Ctenanthe*), *C. insignis, C. louisae* and *C. zebrina* are also good, and *C. ornata* has improbable pink lines on a bronze leaf. They are not easy in ordinary rooms but are ideal plants for a bottle garden. They need shade and a compost with additional peat. Water freely June to August, keep dryer at other times. Re-pot annually if vigorous growth is made and feed in warm weather. P., division.

Calceolaria See *Florists' Plants*.

Campanula isophylla (2) This almost hardy harebell will produce its 1-in. blue or white flowers for many months, and is easily grown in fairly cool, humid conditions, best out of strong sun, and freely watered. It is pendulous and is good in a basket. In winter it needs to be kept dryish in a cool, frost-free place. P., cuttings in spring, easy.

Carex (1) The sedges provide one house plant, *C. morrowii* (syn. *japonica*) *variegata*, often

(Below)
Columnea microphylla makes a spectacular trailing plant, with orange-scarlet flowers; but it is difficult to care for, needing warm, humid conditions

labelled *elegantissima*, a plant with small, narrow flag-iris leaves in tufts, with a white line along each edge. A water plant, it needs to be kept wet. P., division.

Cast Iron Plant See *Aspidistra elatior*.

Castor Oil Plant See *Fatsia*.

Ceropegia (1) *C. woodii* (Hearts Entangled) is an attractive little plant with trailing, twining stems and small fleshy, mottled, heart-shaped leaves to ½ in. across. It prefers a fairly light, moderately warm position, and may produce

its small, tubular purple flowers in a warm room. P., cuttings, or rooting the little tubers formed at the joints.

Chamaedorea See *Neanthe*.

Chestnut Vine See *Tetrastigma voinieriana*.

Chinese Evergreen See *Aglaonema*.

Chlorophytum (syn., *Anthericum*) (1) The Spider Plants form large rosettes of narrow, pale green leaves, 1–2 ft. long. The variegated forms of *C. comosum* and, to a lesser extent, *C. capense* (syn. *elatum*), with wide cream

(Left)
Hoya carnosa variegata is a climber with beautiful glossy leaves, often with a pink tinge. It appreciates some form of support

(Below)
Guzmania cardinalis minor, with its strap-like leaves and red centre, is a member of the Pineapple Family

(Right)
This delightful basket arrangement has contrast of form and colour. It includes monstera, *Cordyline terminalis, Impatiens petersiana, Begonia rex* and *Scindapsus* Marble Queen

stripes on the leaves, are usually grown. The small white flowers appear on long arching stems which later, in *C. comosum*, produce leaf rosettes, giving a graceful 'waterfall' effect. A very tolerant plant for cool or warm rooms, which likes adequate summer watering and feeding, and will stand some shade. P., division, or by rooting plantlets while still on the parent.

Christmas Cactus See *Schlumbergera*.
Cineraria See *Florists' Plants*.

Cissus (1) Tendril climbers closely related to the vines. *C. antarctica*, the Kangaroo Vine, is one of the toughest room plants; it has notched, roughly oval 2-in. leaves. It prefers a cool room and adequate light, especially in winter, but will stand both shade and sun as well as fumes. P., cuttings of 1-year wood in slight heat, easy. Will also root in water. See also *Rhoicissus*, a close relation.

Citrus (2) Orange and lemon trees make attractive plants for cool, airy conditions; in a

warm room they may lose their leaves. Though it is very easy to grow such plants from pips, the seedlings are unlikely to flower: plants bought are usually grafted, and will be in a flowering state. They may even carry fruit! *Citrus mitis* is a small-growing species with miniature oranges 1 in. across. Feed well.

Clivia (1) *C. miniata,* the Kaffir Lily, grown for its many red or orange flowers which are carried on a thick stem in winter, has strap-shaped, dark green leaves, 18 in. long and 2 in. wide, arranged in two rows. It will flower regularly if freely watered in summer and kept fairly dry from November to January, when the temperature should be 7°C. (45°F.). It hates being moved, and can be kept in the same pot for several years, being topdressed each spring and fed in summer. It is an ugly plant out of flower, and if it cannot be placed in the background of a large display is best put outside in summer. It will grow and flower in the shade, but prefers some light, though not full sun. P., offsets.

Clog Plant See *Hypocyrta glabra.*

Cobaea scandens (Cup-and-saucer Vine) See *Annuals.*

Cocos (1) *C. weddeliana,* also known as *Syagrus weddeliana,* is a relation of the Coconut Palm, small plants of which, grown from seeds, are often sold in very small pots. Its stiff much-divided fronds radiate from the base, and it is a useful contrast to more solid leaves, and valuable in a bottle garden. Cultivation, see *Palms.*

Codiaeum variegatum pictum (syn., Croton) (4) Numerous varieties exist with brightly coloured leaves, green, red, yellow, purplish, etc., with many curious shapes and twists. They are difficult plants needing steady, warm, humid conditions, no draughts, no strong sun and plenty of water. Leaf dropping will occur if anything is not to their liking. Good in indoor greenhouses, and very attractive and colourful if they settle down. The narrow-leaved varieties are much easier in rooms than the others. They grow eventually to several feet. P., cuttings in a heated propagating case.

Coleus See *Florists' Plants.*

Collinia See *Neanthe.*

Columnea (4) Mainly trailing plants with attractive paired leaves and spectacular, tubular, two-lipped orange or red flowers, sometimes offered as house plants; but only really suitable for a warm, moist indoor greenhouse. They may survive in a room but are unlikely to flower again. Provide compost with extra peat; diffused light; take care not to under- or over-water. P., cuttings in heat.

Convolvulus See *Annuals.*

Cordyline and Dracaena (2, 3) These two genera are so similar and so much confused that they are best treated under one heading, and are usually known as *Dracaena* in the trade. Dracaenas are also sometimes called Dragon Plants. Cordylines may be differentiated since they have a creeping rootstock. These plants usually have long, arching leaves arranged spirally up a long stem; old specimens will grow very tall. There are many species and varieties, in which the leaves are variously striped and coloured in yellow, silver, purple and red, or a mixture of these. Some, like the nearly hardy *C. australis* and *C. indivisa* (2) have palm-like leaves. They are very striking plants, quite easy to grow if some heat is available, with plenty of water and light and regular syringing. In winter they can be kept at 13–16°C. (55–60°F.), rather dry and well ventilated without draughts. *C. terminalis, D. deremensis, D. fragrans* and *D. sanderiana* (3) are intermediate in heat requirements, as is *D. godseffiana* (3), which has yellow-spotted laurel-like leaves. *D. goldieana* (3) prefers warmth and has bold white markings. All like peat-based composts. P., seed in spring or cuttings (pieces of stem with a bud, or the top

of an old plant will be best), all in moist heat.
Crassula See *Succulents*.
Croton See *Codiaeum*.
Cryptanthus (2) A small genus of dwarf bromeliads, also known as Earth Stars, which form flattened, wavy rosettes of leaves, usually 6–9 in. long, 1–1½ in. wide, which resemble starfishes; the white or green flowers are densely clustered in the centre. They are usually banded or mottled, grey in *C. zonatus,* buff and red in *C. bivittatus,* pink and white in *C. beuckeri. C. undulatus* is a miniature with 2-in. leaves. *C. bromelioides tricolor* is spectacular with cream, green and pink leaves, but also the most tender. All are first rate for bottle gardens. Cultivation, see *Bromeliads*.

Cyclamen (3) These florists' plants with their pink, red or white flowers and often nicely marbled leaves, are sold in immense quantities every winter – and how few survive any length of time. The best advice is to buy the plant early in the autumn, when it should acclimatise successfully and ought to go on flowering steadily. Cyclamens need warm, humid conditions, complete absence of draughts and regular watering. Avoid wetting the top of the corm or rotting of the stems may occur. The plant may with advantage be plunged into damp peat or moss in a bowl; or stood on a block of wood in a saucer, which may be filled with boiling water daily. Keep in a light place.

Cyclamens can be grown on from year to year. When the foliage begins to die down in early summer, dry the pot off gradually, give a few weeks of almost complete dryness, and in August re-pot in a compost with plenty of leafmould or peat and start watering again, gradually increasing the amount. The florists' cyclamen is botanically *C. persicum;* the hardy species cannot be grown indoors.
Cyperus (1) Water plants with long stiff stems crowned by short radiating leaves, hence the common name Umbrella Plant. Easy in moderately warm rooms, in small pots which

(Below)
Dizygotheca elegantissima **is an elegant but temperamental house plant. It needs constant warmth without draughts and careful watering**

41

(Below)
Hypocyrta glabra shows its glossy leaves to advantage against the rich mahogany tones of this table

(Bottom)
Here again *Maranta leuconeura erythrophylla* is placed as the focal point of a sideboard arrangement. The leaves close up at night

(Right)
Impatiens petersiana, a very striking Busy Lizzie with red-purple leaves, is a bushy species useful for small rooms

should stand in a saucer always full of water. Semi-shade. *C. alternifolius, C. diffusus* and their variegated forms are grown. They are 1–2 ft. tall. P., division; leaf-rosettes will root in soil or water.

Cyrtomium falcatum (1) The Holly Fern has stiff fronds up to 2 ft. long, bearing very dark, leathery, toothed pinnae (leaflets) up to 5 in. long. Very easy, tolerating quite dark corners, and should never be put in bright light; it likes more water than most ferns. There is a rare pendulous variety. Cultivation, see *Ferns*.

Cytisus canariensis See *Florists' Plants*.

Date Palm See *Phoenix dactylifera*.

Davallia (2) The main interest in these ferns lies in the furry rhizomes which are formed at soil level and may creep over the pot edge; hence the names Squirrel's-foot Fern *(D. bullata)* and Hare's-foot Fern *(D. canariensis)*. The 1–1½-ft. fronds are finely divided. They need some warmth. Cultivation, see under *Ferns*.

Dieffenbachia (2) Fleshy plants, mostly varieties of *D. picta,* with pointed, oblong leaves up to 1 ft. long, which may be spotted or banded with white or yellow. They prefer constant heat and humidity, with regular spraying, a compost with additional peat, and partial shade, but often settle down in rooms. They will grow several feet tall. P., top cuttings or pieces of stem with buds, in moist heat. Caution: the sap will cause great pain if it reaches the mouth – hence the popular names Dumb Cane and – unkind thought – Mother-in-law Plant.

Dizygotheca (3) Long-stemmed plants, up to 3 ft. with narrow, toothed leaflets in wheel-spoke arrangement at the tips, generally dark green with prominent midrib, reddish in *D. elegantissima* and white in *D. veitchii.* Elegant but temperamental plants, needing constant warmth, peat-based compost, good light, no draughts and careful watering. Small,

well-drained pots are best. Used to be called *Aralia*. P., cuttings in heat.

Dracaena See *Cordyline*.

Dragon Plant Name for *Dracaena*.

Dumb Cane See *Dieffenbachia*.

Easter Cactus See *Rhipsalidopsis*.

Epiphyllum (2) The almost spineless Orchid Cacti, with long flat or triangular joints – 6–12 in. long and 1 in. across – are quite ornamental and will produce their spectacular, variously coloured flowers in a warm room. They need porous, peaty compost, plenty of summer feeding, watering freely in summer and moderately in winter, and shade from bright sun. There are many hybrids. P., cuttings, easy.

Erica See *Florists' Plants*.

Eucalyptus See *Annuals*.

Euphorbia (2, 3) House plants in this huge genus are woody, sub-succulent, spiny species, *E. splendens* (syn. *milii*) (2) and *E. bojeri* (2), which produce small apple-green leaves and bright scarlet flowers at intervals throughout the year. They make bushes 3 ft. through eventually. Treat as succulents (page 60), in full sun and without much water. They need some winter warmth. P., cuttings, allow to dry out for 10 days before insertion. Caution: the milky juice is poisonous.

Euphorbia pulcherrima (3), the Poinsettia, is a beautiful winter-flowering florists' plant, grown for its handsome scarlet, cream or pink bracts and attractively shaped leaves. It needs to be kept light, warm and draught-free, and watered carefully. The Mikkelsen varieties are much tougher than most of the others. When the bracts fade, dry the plant off gradually. Keep dry until May, when cut back hard: begin watering again, and feed, or re-pot. It will reach 2–3 ft. high. P., cuttings in heat.

Fatshedera lizei (1) An attractive hardy plant, a cross between *Fatsia japonica* and *Hedera hibernica* (an ivy), bearing five-pointed, ivy-like leaves, 4–10 in. across, all the way up the upright stems which will grow to several feet. It likes a cool to fairly warm, rather shady place and compost with extra peat, and will tolerate gas and oil fumes. If the leaves drop off, the top should be cut off and re-rooted; the base will sprout again and pieces of stem will also root readily. If bushy growth is preferred, pinch the growing tip. There is a slower-growing, more tender variegated form.

Fatsia japonica (syn., *Aralia japonica*, *A. sieboldii*) (1) An almost hardy plant, with dark, glossy, multi-lobed 6–16-in. leaves, which will in time make a long trunk or can be kept bushy by pinching. Best kept cool and shady; likes fairly frequent feeding and plenty of water. There are yellow and white variegated forms. Makes an impressive specimen. Often mis-called the Castor Oil Plant. P., cuttings.

Ferns (1, 3) Ferns are as varied in shape as any other class of plants. It is mainly those with 'hard' foliage that withstand room conditions best; the delicate kinds, such as the maidenhairs (*Adiantum*), are less satisfactory. Ferns are moisture-lovers; they must have moisture-retaining soil, and preferably a damp, equable atmosphere. They hate draughts. Though they dislike strong sun, they should have some light. Some are hardy and will grow in cold rooms; others can be found to suit various temperatures. Peaty or soil-less composts are best. Drainage should be good and the soil should never be allowed to dry out, but overwatering must be avoided in winter. Re-potting should be carried out, when necessary, in spring. Feeding should be done sparingly if at all. Propagation, in rooms, is by division, which should be done with care.

Details of the following suitable ferns are given in this list: *Adiantum, Asplenium, Cyrtomium, Davallia, Phyllitis, Platycerium* and *Pteris. Blechnum gibbum, Polypodium aureum* and *Pellaea rotundifolia* are also worth growing if available.

Ficus (2, 3) The large fig genus gives us numerous good house plants. *F. elastica* (2) is the well-known India Rubber Plant, with shiny ovate 6–12-in. leaves on an upright stem. *F. e. decora* (2) is a better form with larger leaves held more upright, with dark-red undersides; *F. e. tricolor* (2) has dark and light green and yellow variegation, and *F. e. schryvereana* (2) is cream-patterned. These are easy plants once acclimatised, growing to a large size, preferring warm but standing cool conditions (never below 7°C. [45°F.]) and semi-shade. *F. lyrata* (syn., *F. pandurata*) (3) is similar in habit but has very large, pale green 'waisted' leaves, for which it is sometimes called the Fiddle-leaf Fig. Its leaves will fall if the temperature fluctuates, or the water is too cold or contains chlorine; it needs good winter warmth. *F. benghalensis* (3), the Banyan, has large oval leaves, covered with reddish felt, difficult to clean. *F. benjamina* (2) makes an attractive pendulous shrub or small tree; it has glossy 2–4-in. leaves like those of a willow, the young ones apple-green. *F. australis* (2) is a shrub, with 3-in. rounded leaves, brown underneath; there is a variegated form. *F. diversifolia* (2) is a rather more contorted shrub with 1–3-in. leaves and small round fruits which are carried continuously in a warm room. *F. microphylla* is similar. All these shrubby species may be propagated by leaf or stem cuttings in much heat.

F. pumila (syn., *F. repens*) (2) is a virtually hardy climber with thin woody stems and close-set ¾-in. leaves, with aerial rootlets which cling to any rough surface in a moist atmosphere, though it can be grown as a trailer. It grows rapidly and needs water all the time, regular feeding and shade. There are a variegated and a miniature form. *F. radicans* (2) and its silver-variegated form have rather larger leaves and are a little more choosy. They are suitable for bottle gardens.

Peaty compost containing some sand should

(Below)
Fatshedera lizei is an attractive cross between two genera, *Fatsia* and *Hedera*. A hardy plant, it will tolerate gas and oil fumes. This is the variegated form

be used for all ficuses but potting into too large a pot easily leads to overwatering and failure. On the other hand, the plants should never be allowed to dry right out, especially *F. benjamina*. Young leaves should be protected from sun.

F. elastica varieties may grow enormous. Air layering (see page 10) will re-root the top and new growth will follow below; or the plants can simply be cut back in April. P., otherwise by stem cuttings in much heat.

Fiddle-leaf Fig See *Ficus lyrata*.

Fishbone Plant See *Maranta leuconeura massangeana*.

Fittonia (4) Pretty, low-growing plants with 2–4-in. oval leaves which have either white veins *(F. argyroneura)* or red *(F. verschaffeltii)*. Difficult except in an indoor greenhouse or bottle garden, needing warmth and humidity, shade, and careful watering. Draughts mean death. P., cuttings in heat.

Flamingo Flower See *Anthurium scherzerianum*.

Florists' Plants Under this heading come the following plants which are sold when in flower, and which are usually much best treated as 'expendable', and discarded when the flowers are over, especially as many are ugly when out of bloom. Of these *Azalea, Cyclamen* and *Euphorbia pulcherrima* (Poinsettia) are dealt with in the List. *Astilbe* (Spiraea) and *Hydrangea* can be put in the garden after flowering. *Calceolaria, Cineraria, Erica* and *Solanum* are best discarded unless a greenhouse is available. *Coleus, Cytisus canariensis* and *Primula obconica* may survive a long time; *Fuchsia* needs a winter rest, almost dry. *Gloxinia, Gesneria* and *Smithiantha* are very showy warm greenhouse plants which must have heat and humidity: they may not live long. For *Kalanchoë blossfeldiana* and *Crassula (Rochea) coccinea*, see *Succulents*.

These plants have all been grown in greenhouses in conditions vastly different from

(Left)
Neanthe elegans is a dwarf palm which makes a very elegant plant, with leaves from 8–16 ins. long, in quite cool conditions

(Below)
This philodendron, named Burgundy, is growing on a mossed stake, which aids its growth. It makes a striking coffee table plant

(Bottom)
These house plants have been selected carefully to complement the colours of their setting. With care a pleasing effect can be achieved

those of the room that they will go to. Many of them are winter flowering, and may suffer a death-dealing check between leaving the greenhouse and being bought by the customer – before in fact the customer has any control over the plant. The remarks on acclimatisation (page 6) are therefore to be taken even more strongly than with permanent plants, and if winter-flowering, the earlier they can be bought in autumn the better.

Most of these plants prefer fairly cool, airy conditions, as they need a lot of air humidity, and – in particular those needing some warmth – will benefit by frequent syringing and being stood above water as described on page 4. None of them like full sunshine, but they do need light.

Friendship Plant See *Pilea*.

Fuchsia See *Florists' Plants*.

Genista See *Florists' Plants*.

Geranium See *Pelargonium*.

Gesneria and Gloxinia See *Florists' Plants*.

Grape Ivy See *Rhoicissus rhomboidea*.

Grevillea robusta (2) The Silk Oak is really a tree with 9–12-in., finely cut, fern-like silvery leaves. Young plants raised from seeds are grown indoors, where they will soon make big specimens. It likes cool, fairly light conditions and ample summer waterings; it will drop leaves if allowed to dry out. If this happens, the top should be cut off and rooted in slight heat. Otherwise propagate by seed.

Guzmania (2) A large genus of bromeliads, very brilliantly coloured in the centre when in flower, and forming spreading rosettes. Cultivation, see *Bromeliads*.

Hare's-foot Fern See *Davallia canariensis*.

Hart's-tongue Fern
See *Phyllitis scolopendrium*.

Hearts Entangled See *Ceropegia woodii*.

Heaths See *Erica* under *Florists' Plants*.

Hedera (2) The ivies are adaptable house plants, available in a very wide range of leaf shapes, sizes and variegations. Most are

(Below)
Monstera deliciosa **is a striking architectural plant with large, perforated leaves and thick aerial roots**

climbers, which may be used as trailers, and a few have stiff, compact growth (e.g. *H. helix conglomerata*). Most ivies produce long single 'trails', but there are self-branching sorts such as Adam, Chicago, Green Ripple, Heisse, Little Diamond and Lutzii, which make bushier plants. In warm rooms it is perhaps better to use *H. canariensis* and its varieties, rather than the British *H. helix* and its forms, which are very hardy and should be kept cool – below 10°C. (50°F.) in winter. All need to be moist both at the roots and over the foliage – dry air is their worst enemy, plus red spider. A good spraying once a week is beneficial. Keep on the dry side in winter. They prefer a certain amount of shade but the variegated forms need some light, especially that of *H. canariensis*. P., tip cuttings; will root in water.

Helxine soleirolii (1) Mind-your-own-business or Baby's Tears makes trailing stems, clothed with tiny pale green or gold leaves. It should always be kept moist, preferably by standing the pot in a saucer of water; water is best kept off the foliage. It is wisest to keep it to itself, for it will root into other pots very readily and may become a nuisance. It is nearly hardy and will grow anywhere, but hates dry air. P., division.

Hibiscus (4) Though the exotic *H. rosa-sinensis* could be grown in a warm indoor greenhouse, it would take a lot of room. The variety *cooperi* is sometimes sold as a foliage plant, for its narrow leaves are variegated with white, pink, red and dark green. In an ordinary room it can only be regarded as temporary. P., cuttings in heat.

Holly Fern See *Cyrtomium falcatum*.

House Lime See *Sparmannia*.

Howea See *Kentia*.

Hoya (1) Plants with thick, glossy, dark, oval 1½–3-in. leaves, which will stand cool conditions and flower in warm, moist ones. The flowers are small, scented, wax-like (hence the name Wax Flower) and in clusters.

The leaves, which are sometimes white-spotted, are quite decorative alone. Though the plants are naturally climbers with small aerial roots, the stems are strong enough to make a bushy effect on small specimens. They prefer semi-shade, compost with additional peat, plenty of water, good drainage, and must not be potted into too large a pot. Keep at 10°C. (50°F.) in winter. If flowers are produced give less water. Do not cut off old flower stems, as new flowering growths are produced there. *H. carnosa* and the larger *H. australis* are the easiest to grow. *H. carnosa* has a variegated form. *H. bella* is dwarf and pendulous, has prettier flowers and needs more heat. P., cuttings in heat.

Hydrangea hortensis See *Florists' Plants*.

Hypocyrta (2) Plants related to *Columnea* and needing the same cultivation, with thick, glossy leaves and pouch-shaped flowers, red in *H. nummularia,* orange-yellow in *H. glabra,* the Clog Plant. The latter has dark foliage and will stand cool conditions, especially if kept fairly dry. P., cuttings in heat.

Impatiens (2) The Busy Lizzies – *I. holstii, I. sultanii* and hybrids – are fleshy-stemmed plants, 1–2 ft. high, which produce 1½-in. pink, red or white flowers continuously in rather warm, moist conditions. There are also 6-in. dwarf strains. *I. petersiana* is a very striking plant with deep red-purple foliage and bright red flowers; it grows taller and is a little more difficult to manage. All these plants are easily grown in summer, when they should be watered and fed very freely, but tend to become leggy and damp off in winter, when they must be kept warm, very light and rather dry. Pinch back for bushiness. Cuttings strike very easily, even in water, and a stock should be rooted in early autumn to provide good plants by next spring. Seed sown in heat also produces flowering plants quickly.

India Rubber Plant See *Ficus elastica*.

Ipomoea (Morning Glory) See *Annuals*.

Philodendron scandens, with heart-shaped leaves, is one of the easiest of the philodendrons to grow and eventually makes a tall plant

Ivy See the reference to *Hedera*.

Jasminum (2) *J. polyanthum* is sometimes sold as a pot plant for its deliciously-scented white flowers and graceful foliage. Though easy enough to keep alive it is difficult to bring it into flower again without a greenhouse or conservatory. It is nearly hardy and must be kept cool and airy. P., cuttings.

Kaffir Lily See *Clivia*.

Kalanchoë See *Succulents*.

Kangaroo Vine See *Cissus antarctica*.

Kentia (syn., *Howea*) (1) Palms of the easiest cultivation with flat, slender, hanging leaves up to 4 ft. long. *K. forsteriana* is quick growing; *K. belmoreana* is slower, but hardier and more attractive. Both reach a considerable height. Cultivation, see *Palms*.

Lemon See *Citrus*.

Maidenhair Fern See *Adiantum*.

Maranta (3) Pretty, low-growing plants; the commonly grown *M. leuconeura kerchoveana* has oblong, 6-in. apple-green leaves with two rows of diamond-shaped markings, which are purple on young leaves and go brown later. The leaves close together at night, which gives it the name Prayer Plant. The variety *M. l. massangeana* has regular white veins on a dark green background, and is known as the Fishbone Plant. A newer variety is *M. l. erythrophylla* or *tricolor*, with large yellowish-green leaves, which have dark red veins and deep green blotches. Marantas need heat and moist air, but will acclimatise to cooler conditions if kept in a constant atmosphere out of draughts. Several other species are well worth growing. They are all admirable for bottle gardens. See *Calathea* for cultivation and other species.

Maurandya See *Annuals*.

Mind-your-own-business See under *Helxine soleirolii*.

Monstera deliciosa (2) A striking plant with large, perforated, heart-shaped leaves and long, thick aerial roots, which soon becomes very large. Unfortunately, though it will grow well in a shady, quite cool room, it needs a free root-run if it is to produce well perforated leaves. Even in a large pot the leaves are often plain or have only one or two holes or cuts. Really old, well-grown plants have double or triple rows of holes in leaves up to 18 in. wide, but the ones in commerce usually only have one set of holes and are about 9 in. wide. The faster-climbing immature form, with large heart-shaped leaves and few holes, is sometimes called *Philodendron pertusum*. Use compost with additional peat and feed well. Allow nearly to dry out between waterings. Keep out of draughts and fluctuating temperatures or the leaves go brown. If the plant grows leggy, cut off the top and root it in much heat, or carry out air layering. The plant will stand cutting back hard if it grows too tall. Sometimes called the Swiss Cheese Plant. P., cuttings (top of shoot with a mature leaf).

Mother-in-law's Tongue See *Sansevieria*.

Mother of Thousands See under *Saxifraga sarmentosa*.

Natal Vine See *Rhoicissus*.

Neanthe elegans (syn., *N. bella, Chamaedorea elegans*; the latest name is *Collinia elegans*) (1) A miniature palm, eventually up to 3 ft., with graceful foliage 1–2 ft. long, but usually much smaller, which is easy to grow in almost any conditions. Useful as a contrast in bottle gardens, it needs little feeding, and will stand dry air and fumes. Cultivation, see *Palms*.

Neoregelia (2) A large genus of bromeliads, many of them, such as *N. spectabilis*, with brightly coloured tips to the leaves, which earn them the name Painted Fingernail Plants. The best known is *N. carolinae tricolor*, with a large, flat rosette striped with cream and pink. Cultivation, see *Bromeliads*.

Nephthytis See *Syngonium*.

Nidularium (2) Attractive bromeliads with low, spreading 'leaf-vase' rosettes which go red around the centre when the flowers are produced there. *N. fulgens* and *N. rutilans* have 12-in. mottled leaves, 2 in. broad; *N. innocentii* has 8-in. by 2-in. leaves, reddish purple below. Cultivation, see *Bromeliads*.

Norfolk Island Pine See *Araucaria excelsa*.

Oplismenus hirtellus (syn., *Panicum variegatum*) (2) A grass with 1–3 in. flat leaves pointed at each end. In the variety *albidus* they are white with a green midrib; in the variety *variegatus* they are striped white and pink. They need some warmth, lots of water, will tolerate a certain amount of shade but need light in winter. Good for edgings; renew fairly often to maintain a good appearance. P., cuttings, very easy.

Orange See *Citrus*.

Orchid Cacti See *Epiphyllum*.

Painted Fingernail Plant See *Neoregelia*.

Palms Many palms are well adapted to cultivation indoors, having stiff, tough foliage, and do not grow too large if kept in large pots or tubs. They prefer damp air; if the air is dry or the plants are in draughts, the leaf tips will go brown. The leaves should be sponged regularly. They will stand sun, but are best in indirect light. They need adequate water in summer, little in winter, and may remain in the same containers till quite pot-bound; they should be fed in summer and topdressed annually. A good potting mixture contains 3 parts of fibrous loam, 1 part of leafmould, 1 part of cow manure, 1 part of coarse sand; a little bonemeal may be added. Potting should be very firm. Propagation is usually from seed, which germinates readily in moist heat; also by division or suckers. Details of the following palms are given in this List: *Cocos, Kentia (Howea), Phoenix*, and the most attractive for rooms, *Neanthe*.

Pandanus (2) The screw pines – palm-like plants with long, narrow, very spiny, recurving leaves arranged in a spiral. In *P. utilis* the spines are reddish; in *P. veitchii* the

leaves have white stripes. Need light and fair winter warmth, free summer watering and occasional spraying. They like compost with additional peat and can remain in the same smallish pot for several years. At first making a rosette, they eventually reach a considerable height with corkscrew-marked trunks. P., suckers in some heat.

Panicum See *Oplismenus*.

Passiflora See under *Annuals*.

Peacock Plant See *Calathea makoyana*.

Pelargonium (2) The familiar zonal and semi-pendulous ivy-leaved 'geraniums' so much used for summer bedding will flower in a well-lit window. Some zonal varieties have strikingly coloured leaves. If prevented from flowering in summer, they will do so in autumn and winter. The beautiful regal pelargoniums need warmer conditions, and flower for a short season only. None of these types seem to fit in very well with most house plants – the scented-leaved kinds are the most suitable. These are smaller shrubby plants, many having delicately-shaped and variegated leaves with a variety of delicious scents when touched, and small but attractive white, pink or purple flowers. All pelargoniums must have full sunlight or they become very leggy.

All types need some feeding and copious summer watering, and winter rest in cool but frost-free conditions. In early spring they may be re-potted and also cut back if desired. Zonals, especially, are best raised afresh each year to have nice-looking plants. Cuttings root readily in sandy loam, kept moderately moist; take them in spring or August if possible. The scented-leaved kinds need only smallish pots; the others fairly large ones.

Pellionia (3) *P. daveauana* has grey-green leaves edged with dark olive green; *P. pulchra* has attractive veining. They are useful as colour contrasts, and being low, creeping plants, can be striking hanging over the edge of a white container. They need compost with extra peat and a warm, even temperature, avoiding dry or stuffy air. P., cuttings in heat.

Peperomia (3) A huge genus of low-growing, bushy, often fleshy plants; most have attractively patterned leaves (usually 2–3 in. long) and many have pink or red stems. Flowers may be produced in warm, moist conditions – they usually look like rats' tails – but the plants will acclimatise to cooler conditions so long as they are kept out of draughts and not watered with very cold water, or overwatered in winter. Nor must they be hot and dry. They need light but not strong sun. *P. magnoliaefolia* has cream and pale green leaves; *P. obtusifolia* has large, fleshy purple-margined leaves; *P. caperata* has small corrugated leaves and white flowers; *P. glabella* is trailing, with dark green leaves; *P. scandens* is similar, but white-marked, and creeps or climbs; *P. hederaefolia* has greyish markings. *P. sandersii* (syn., *P. argyreia*) is the most decorative, with silver crescents on 4–5-in. round leaves; it is a little more difficult than most. *P. nummularifolia* and *P. microphylla* have small leaves on trailing stems. There are numerous other species which are sometimes available. Re-pot seldom but feed occasionally. Useful for bottle gardens. P., leaf or stem cuttings in heat.

Philodendron (1, 3) This is one of the most important house plant genera, and the number of species in cultivation increases steadily. Many are vigorous climbers with aerial roots; thus they can be grown up mossy branches or wire cylinders filled with moss. The leaves are glossy, leathery, and in a wide variety of shapes. They are quick growing and mainly tolerant of quite difficult conditions, though they prefer warmth and humidity. They like shade, dislike draughts, and need compost with extra peat, and summer feeding. Do not pot them into too large a pot.

The commonest climbing species grown is *P. scandens* (1), the Sweetheart Vine, with heart-shaped 2–6-in. leaves. *P. erubescens* (1) has long-oval to arrow-head 7–12 in. leaves. Burgundy (3) is a striking hybrid with shining blackish-green leaves and red stems. *P. hastatum* (1) has 7-in. spear-head leaves and makes a fine specimen. *P. oxycardium* (1) has narrower 9–12-in. leaves. *P. laciniatum* (1) is deeply notched in a grotesque manner. *P. radiatum* (1) is similar but more regular, and *P. elegans* (1) has very deeply cut leaves. *P. panduriforme (bipennifolium)* (1) has 6–9-in., 5-lobed leaves of indescribable shape; while *P. leichtlinii* (3) has 9–12-in. oblong leaves, very much perforated like *Monstera*, but paler and of much thinner texture. It is more difficult than the other species, as are *P. andreanum* (3) and *P. melanochrysum* (3), which are velvety, and with rosy young foliage.

Then there is a group of non-climbers, which radiate leaves from a central crown at ground level, including the deeply indented *P. selloum, P. pinnatifidum* and *P. bipinnatifidum* (the last is a very tolerant plant, and the only one usually grown), all with leaves up to 12–24 in. long, and the plain-margined *P. wendlandii*, with narrow 12–24 in. leaves and curious swollen leaf-stalks. *P. pertusum* is the juvenile form of *Monstera deliciosa* (page 50). P., layering, or cuttings (including plant tops) in much heat; non-climbers from seed in moderate heat.

Phoenix (2) *Phoenix dactylifera* is the Date Palm, which has narrow, elegant, bluish 8–16-in. leaves. It will stand quite cool, airy conditions, as will *P. canariensis*, which has very long green foliage and makes a massive crown. *P. rupicola* is normally grown; it has a rare variegated form. These all reach a considerable height. *P. roebelinii* is dwarf, only reaching 5 ft. at most, and is more graceful, but needs warmer conditions.

Date stones can be grown; place one in a pot of peaty, sandy compost, cover with a piece of glass or a jar, and keep damp and as warm as possible till germination occurs. Keep the seedling warm until it is well developed. It takes some time to look anything like a palm! Cultivation, see *Palms*.

Phyllitis scolopendrium (syn., *Scolopendrium vulgare*) (1) The Hart's-tongue Fern, with glossy strap-shaped 6–18-in. fronds, and its numerous varieties, with crisped or wavy edges and ends cut or feathered in many ways, are excellent and attractive plants in cool or cold rooms in shade. They are quite hardy. Cultivation, see *Ferns*.

Pick-a-back Plant See *Tolmiea menziesii*.

Pilea (2) *P. cadierei* is an attractive plant with 2–4-in. oval leaves embossed with regular aluminium markings. In America it is aptly called the Aluminium Plant. For some obscure reason it is also known as the Friendship Plant. There is a dwarf form which is useful in bottle gardens and needs little stopping to make it bushy. *P. involucrata* has roundish 'gilded' leaves in copper and silver. *P.* Bronze, or Silver Tree, appears to be a distinct species, with rounder, larger leaves, pale bronze with a central silver band. It also is a valuable bottle plant. Bushy, with erect stems, all these plants prefer rather warm, moist, shady conditions, plenty of water and feeding. Dryness and draughts make them lose leaves. *P. cadierei* will acclimatise to cool conditions. *P. nummularifolia* is a hanging plant with ¾-in. round leaves. P., cuttings, easy.

Platycerium (2) The stag's-horn ferns are bizarre and striking plants. They are epiphytes, with large, rounded fronds which clasp the tree-trunk on which they grow. The fertile fronds are like flattened antlers up to 2 ft. long, of an attractive grey-green. *P. bifurcatum* is the usual species grown; the very similar *P. alcicorne* is also in commerce. These are best grown either on a flat pan or on top of a basket containing peat and leafmould, which the clasping fronds can envelop; or on a

mass of osmunda fibre wired to a wood block. Water freely whenever the fronds begin to droop. Do not let water remain on the fronds or lodge in the centre. It is advisable to buy a reasonably large, well-hardened specimen, which will stand quite low winter temperatures (minimum 4°C. [40°F.]), though it prefers some warmth. It likes good light, but not sun, and very free-draining peaty compost; seldom re-pot; do not spray leaves.

Plectranthus (2) Easy plants with fleshy, heart-shaped, notched 2–3-in. leaves with marked veins and sprawling brittle stems. *P. fruticosus* has green, shiny leaves; *P. oertendahlii* has downy leaves, dark purple beneath. They need cool, light, airy conditions and compost with extra peat. P., cuttings in heat, easy.

Poinsettia See *Euphorbia pulcherrima*.

Pothos See *Scindapsus*.

Prayer Plant See *Maranta leuconeura kerchoveana*.

Primula See *Florists' Plants*.

Pteris (1) Very easy ferns which will stand hard treatment, characterised by pale green, ribbon-like, forking fronds. The usual species grown is *P. cretica*, which reaches 9–12 in.; *P. multifida* (syn., *serrulata*) is similar but larger. *P. ensiformis* and *P. biaurita* (syn., *quadriaurita*) are also quite good indoors. There are many varieties which may have wavy, much-divided or feathered fronds, and some with white or grey lines on the fronds. *P. biaurita tricolor* has reddish fronds with silver lines. I find the small specimens of *P. cretica* so often seen in shops rather ugly, but a well-grown specimen, particularly of a striped variety, is quite effective. Water freely. Cultivation, see *Ferns*.

Rhipsalidopsis (1) *R. gaertneri* is the current name for the Easter Cactus, originally called *Schlumbergera gaertneri*. It is a compact pendulous plant with bright red flowers. Cultivation, as for *Schlumbergera*.

(Right)
Pilea cadierei, the Aluminium Plant, has attractive metallic markings on the shapely leaves

(Below)
Pandanus veitchii, has spiny, variegated leaves arranged in a spiral. Mature plants form corkscrew-like trunks

(Below)
A bizarre and striking plant, *Platycerium bifurcatum* **has fronds like antlers and its roots buried in moss, sandwiched between blocks of wood**

(Bottom)
It is in winter that *Schlumbergera buckleyi* **begins to flower. A constant temperature is needed to prevent buds from dropping**

Rhodochiton See the reference to *Annuals*.

Rhoeo discolor (syn., *R. spathacea, Tradescantia discolor*) (3) An attractive plant with rosettes of narrow leaves up to 12 in. long, tapering at each end, rich purple below, which may be variegated with cream and purple above, carried on a short trunk-like stem and giving the appearance of a miniature palm. Flowers are borne at the base in curious boat-shaped bracts. It needs to be carefully acclimatised, liking equable warmth, plenty of water, compost with extra peat, occasional spraying, and shade from sun. P., cuttings.

Rhoicissus rhomboidea (1) The Grape Ivy or Natal Vine, a tendril climber related to the grape vine, with small, dark green, glossy 1-in. leaflets borne in threes. The young shoots are silvery. An easy plant which grows fast and may be grown as a bush, needing cool, airy summer conditions and some warmth in winter. Likes adequate watering and feeding. P., cuttings of fairly old growth, which will root in water, but layering is best.

Rochea See *Crassula* under *Succulents*.

Saintpaulia (3) The African Violet is *the* house plant of America, and it is becoming quite popular elsewhere. It is a pretty little plant with hairy, dark green, oval 1–2-in. leaves radiating from a central crown. There are now hundreds of varieties of *S. ionantha* and other species in which the (ideally) almost continuously produced flowers may be blue, mauve, violet, pink or white, single or double, and the leaves may be mottled or can be variously shaped.

It is, however, a plant for the typical American room, needing a very warm (13°C. [55°F.] at night, 18–21°C. [65–70°F.] by day) and moist atmosphere, and in inadequately heated rooms it is often a dismal failure. It hates draughts, gas, cold water and changes of atmosphere, and succeeds best in an indoor greenhouse. It should be kept out of sun, but needs ample light; growers have fluorescent lighting, often kept on for 12 or 14 hours at a time. The compost should have extra peat, and summer feeding is desirable. Water moderately from below, always with caution, with room-temperature water. Rotting may follow overwatering or any damage. Place the pots if possible in or above a layer of moist peat, or above pebbles with water below. Plastic pots are ideal. P., division; leaf cuttings in peat or water.

Sansevieria (2) The usual species seen is *S. trifasciata*. This odd plant makes clumps of long, twisting, sword-shaped, mottled leaves rising vertically from the ground. The variety *laurentii* is most commonly grown: it is bigger, rising to 3–4 ft., and is margined with yellow. It is sometimes called Snake Plant or Bowstring Hemp, or Mother-in-law's Tongue. It is a sub-succulent desert plant which will stand shade, but prefers sun; a heavy compost is usually recommended but it grows well in soil-less compost; the plant can be allowed to become pot-bound, and should always be watered sparingly, especially in winter, when it needs some warmth. Overwatering is the usual cause of failure; otherwise it is an easy plant. There are other species, including some with cylindrical leaves and some forming rosettes, like the stocky *S. hahni,* which also has a variegated form. P., division; or cuttings, first dried and struck in sand, but these will not reproduce the yellow edges in *laurentii*.

Saxifraga stolonifera (syn., *S. sarmentosa*) (1) A plant of many names, including Mother of Thousands. It has reddish, hairy, marbled leaves, and produces quantities of runners in the same way as a strawberry. A fine array of young plants will soon hang down if the pot is suitably placed. It produces a mass of small pink flowers on long stems in summer. It is hardy and needs cool conditions, a light but not sunny position, and must be kept very moist and fed in summer. The more delicate form, *S. tricolor*, is attractively marked with red and cream variegation. P., runners, easy.

Schefflera (2) A quick-growing, upright shrub related to *Fatsia, S. actinophylla* is a recent introduction with large leathery, glossy, oblong leaflets, each on a distinct stalk and radiating from a central point – hence the name Umbrella Tree. A big plant makes an excellent individual specimen. It prefers shade and a moderately moist atmosphere, and will grow in standard compost. The soil should be allowed partly to dry out before being thoroughly soaked. Re-pot annually. There is a variegated form. P., cuttings.

Schlumbergera (1) The proper name for the Christmas Cactus usually referred to as *Zygocactus. S. buckleyi* and *S. truncata* have 1–2-in. flat, notched, leaf-like segments, jointed together and forking occasionally. The growth is short and pendulous, and they may be grown in a basket. In winter they produce multi-petalled flowers up to 3 in. long and 1 in. across, usually cerise or magenta, but other colour forms exist. They need feeding in summer and watering all the time, though after flowering watering may be restricted for some weeks. In winter they appreciate some warmth, which should be constant; fluctuating temperatures, draughts or drying out will cause any buds to drop. The Easter Cactus is now *Rhipsalidopsis gaertneri* (see page 54). P., cuttings of 2–3 segments, easy.

Scindapsus (syn., *Pothos*) (1) *S. aureus* is very similar to a *Philodendron scandens* in which the leaves are streaked unevenly with a rather virulent yellow. Golden Queen is similar but more attractive; Marble Queen is cream-variegated and a better form. Silver Queen is almost entirely white. *S. pictus argyraeus* is a very attractive plant with silvery markings on thicker, also heart-shaped 4–6-in. leaves. They are all vigorous climbers. Cultivation, as for *Philodendron*.

Scolopendrium vulgare
See *Phyllitis scolopendrium*.

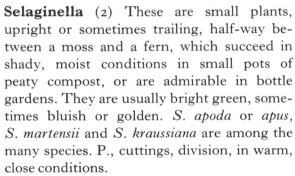

(Left)
The saintpaulia, or African Violet, is one of the most delightful of all the flowering house plants. It will often bloom throughout the year

(Right)
***Scindapsus aureus* is seen here as a trailing plant, but it will also make a vigorous climber**

(Below right)
***Rhoicissus rhomboidea* is one of the hardiest of all house plants. With its vigorous climbing habit, it is a natural choice for a beginner**

Selaginella (2) These are small plants, upright or sometimes trailing, half-way between a moss and a fern, which succeed in shady, moist conditions in small pots of peaty compost, or are admirable in bottle gardens. They are usually bright green, sometimes bluish or golden. *S. apoda* or *apus*, *S. martensii* and *S. kraussiana* are among the many species. P., cuttings, division, in warm, close conditions.

Setcreasea (2) *S. striata* is very like *Zebrina pendula* in shape, but the leaves are pale green with fine parallel white lines. *S. purpurea*, or Purple Heart, has narrow, elongated leaves of rosy purple, and a tendency to sprawl. They are not as easy as *Zebrina*, needing more warmth, and must have good light or they will become spindly. Good light and fairly dry soil also encourage good purple colour in *S. purpurea*. P., cuttings, easy.

Shrimp Plant See *Beloperone guttata*.
Silk Oak See *Grevillea robusta*.
Smilax See *Asparagus asparagoides*.
Smithiantha See *Florists' Plants*.
Snake Plant See *Sansevieria trifasciata*.
Solanum See *Florists' Plants*.
Sparmannia africana (2) This attractive shrub produces pale green, hairy, heart-shaped leaves. It is related to the lime, and is sometimes called House Lime. It will make a very big specimen if allowed to, or may be cut back severely as desired. The leaves will

become quite large – up to 8 in. across in ideal conditions. It needs good light but not bright sun, a great deal of water at all times, and prefers frequent re-potting. It will stand a minimum winter temperature of 7°C. (45°F.). It is sensitive to draughts, dry air, and the soil drying out, when its leaves will go yellow and fall. In a warm, moist atmosphere the white flowers may be produced. P., cuttings in slight heat, easy; will root in water.

Spathiphyllum (2) Arum relations with flowers like a miniature elongated Jack-in-the-pulpit, similar to *Anthurium*, and needing similar treatment, though rather less fussy but not very attractive out of flower. *S. wallisii* had 6-in. white flowers and dark, narrow 6-in. leaves. There are other species. Flowers last for several weeks. Re-pot, feed and divide often.

Spider Plant See *Chlorophytum*.

Spiraea See *Astilbe* under *Florists' Plants*.

Squirrel's-foot Fern See *Davallia bullata*.

Stag's-horn Fern See *Platycerium*.

Succulents These plants, which include cacti, are described in more detail on pages 66 to 128. Most make excellent room plants provided they are given maximum sunlight, and hence can only be kept satisfactorily in a south window, where they should be placed as near to the glass as possible.

Most thrive in dry air, and dislike stuffy, damp conditions. Watering can, in general, be free in summer, but it is always best to err on the dry side or rotting may follow, especially in poor light conditions. In winter the soil should be kept from drying out, no more. A number of small plants can be grown together in shallow pans or bowls, and watering can then be reduced to prevent excessive growth. A winter temperature of 10°C (50°F.) is ample, with a minimum of 4°C. (40°F.). Frost protection is necessary; if the room is cold a few sheets of newspaper between plants and window will suffice. Do not draw the curtains

so as to leave plants between them and the window on cold nights. Avoid draughts.

The soil may be 4 parts of John Innes Potting Compost No. 1 with 1 part of coarse sand and crushed brick and/or vermiculite. Drainage must always be very good. Re-potting should be done when necessary; many of these plants grow quickly. Most are readily propagated from offsets or cuttings, which should be well dried before inserting in coarse sand.

Cacti are almost all spiny, though *Epiphyllum* and *Schlumbergera* are barely so. These have showy flowers and prefer peaty compost, moist air and less sun than most other cacti. *Cephalocereus, Cereus, Chamaecereus, Echinocereus, Echinopsis, Ferocactus* and *Opuntia* make fairly big specimens which mix reasonably well with other house plants, but they take time to attain any size. *Astrophytum, Lobivia, Mammillaria* and *Parodia* are attractive-looking plants which never become very big.

Of other succulents, species of the following are particularly suitable for rooms, as they make fair-sized, decorative plants quite quickly, and fit in with other house plants: *Agave, Aloe, Ceropegia, Crassula, Euphorbia, Kalanchoë* and *Rochea*. Other genera with suitable species are *Aeonium, Cotyledon, Echeveria, Gasteria, Haworthia, Pachyphytum, Sedum* and *Stapelia*, and the free-flowering shrubby mesembryanthemums (*Lampranthus*).

Sweetheart Vine See *Philodendron scandens*.

Swiss Cheese Plant See *Monstera deliciosa*.

Syngonium (1) Quick-growing climbers related to *Philodendron*, with 3–7-lobed arrow-headed, leathery, dark green 6–8-in. leaves, which give the plants the name Goose Foot. Cultivation, as for *Philodendron*. If grown without a climbing support the plants make short-jointed growth, but they are most effective trained over a wire cylinder filled with moss, or on cork bark kept moist, which encourages their prolific aerial roots. *S. podophyllum* and *S. vellozianum* are commonly grown. There is a variegated form of the first which is often called *Nephthytis* Emerald Gem in the house plant trade.

Tetrastigma (3) *T.* (or *Vitis*) *voinerianum* is a rampant tendril climber with 5-lobed, notched leaves, glossy above, brown-felted below, in shape and size like those of a horse chestnut, hence the name Chestnut Vine. The young growths are covered with silvery down. In constant atmospheric conditions growth is rapid. The plant is brittle, and draughts, careless handling and, in particular, overwatering will cause the leaves and stem sections to drop, though it usually grows again from the part left. In Scandinavia, this propensity has earned it the name Lizard Plant! Keep out of full sun. Compost with extra peat and large pots are necessary, and also frequent feeding in summer; keep almost entirely dry in winter. P., cuttings in bottom heat, difficult.

Thunbergia See *Annuals*

Tillandsia (2) One of the largest genera of bromeliads, very variable in shape – *T. usneoides*, the Spanish Moss, has no roots and can grow on telegraph-poles, obtaining moisture from the air. *T. lindeniana* or *lindeni* is sometimes obtainable: it has an arching rosette of narrow, pointed, 15-in. leaves, purple at the base. Many hybrids have been raised, and most tillandsias are worth growing. Cultivation, see *Bromeliads*.

Tolmiea menziesii (1) A low-growing hardy plant making a spreading clump of light green, heart-shaped, hairy, notched 2-in. leaves on long stems, whose main interest lies in the young plants produced on the lower leaves which in nature root as they touch the soil. They give it the common and apt name of Pick-a-back Plant. It is very easy to cultivate, needing some shade and lots of water. P., rooting leaf-buds, even in water.

(Below)
Tradescantia fluminensis variegata has attractive variegation. It will trail and makes an excellent plant for a hanging basket

(Bottom)
If you have a sunny windowsill, cacti and other succulents are an interesting addition to your house plant collection. With care, many can be persuaded to flower

Tradescantia (1–3) Species grown indoors are mainly creeping plants, often called Wandering Jew, with fleshy stems with a leaf at each joint. *T. fluminensis* (1) is a very common plant; it is naturally a glossy, dark green, but there are more attractive forms with white, pink or yellow striping on the 1½-in. leaves. Its stems will grow several feet long. There are a number of similar species which have given rise to special forms like the large silver-striped Quick Silver (2) and the small white-streaked Silver (1). *T. blossfeldiana* (1) is hairy on the thicker stems and the purple undersides of the larger leaves. *T. reginae* (3) is a handsome, erect plant with 6-in. leaves with dark green banding on pale green, purple below: it needs warmth and humidity. *T. sillamontana* (3) is a very beautiful but unfortunately temperamental plant entirely covered in silvery felt. Any other greenhouse species are worth growing. All root very readily at the joints on contact with the soil, and can be rooted in water, and young plants of *T. fluminensis* in particular should be periodically rooted as the parents become too leggy. They are all excellent in baskets and trailing over container edges; they will stand cold but grow better in warmth. Dry air causes the lower leaves to shrivel. See also *Setcreasea* and *Zebrina*.

Trichosporum See *Aeschynanthus*.

Tropaeolum See *Annuals*.

Umbrella Plant See *Cyperus*.

Umbrella Tree See *Schefflera*.

Vriesia (2) A numerous genus of bromeliads, making large rosettes of sculptural appearance. *V. splendens* is often obtainable and has 15-in. leaves, 2½ in. wide, with brownish banding and a long, narrow 'tongue' of scarlet-bracted yellow flowers. *V. hieroglyphica* and *V. tesselata* are bigger, fascinating plants. Cultivation, see *Bromeliads*.

Wandering Jew
See *Tradescantia* and *Zebrina*.

Wax-flower See *Hoya*.

Winter Cherry

See *Solanum* under *Florists' Plants*.

Zebrina pendula (1) A close relation of *Tradescantia* and often confused with it (also known as *T. zebrina*), needing identical cultivation. It has 2–3-in. leaves of glossy green with two bands of silver which sparkle metallically. The undersides are purple and if the plant is kept on the dry side the colouring becomes very rich. There is an unusual variegated form which is very colourful, with cream and reddish streaks added to the silver, but it is quite difficult to grow.

Zygocactus See *Schlumbergera*.

RECOMMENDED PLANTS FOR VARIOUS CONDITIONS

Easy plants Aspidistra, most Cacti, Chlorophytum, *Cissus antarctica,* Clivia, Cyrtomium, Fatshedera, Hoya, Palms, Pteris, Rhoicissus, many Succulents, Tolmiea, Tradescantia, Zebrina.

Other plants for average rooms Acorus, Asparagus, Asplenium, Bromeliads, Carex, Cyperus, Epiphyllum, Fatsia, Ficus, Hedera, Impatiens, most Philodendrons, Platycerium, Plectranthus, Sansevieria, *Saxifraga sarmentosa,* Schefflera, Scindapsus, Schlumbergera, Syngonium.

Plants for central heating Aglaonema, Anthurium, Aspidistra, Begonia, Bromeliads, Cacti, Chlorophytum, Clivia, Cordyline, Cyrtomium, Dieffenbachia, Dracaena, Epiphyllum, Fatshedera, Ficus, Hoya, Palms, Pandanus, Philodendron, Sansevieria, Scindapsus, Schlumbergera, most Succulents, Syngonium, Tradescantia, Zebrina.

Plants to stand shade Acorus, Aglaonema, Anthurium, Aspidistra, Begonia, Bromeliads, Calathea, Carex, Clivia, Codiaeum, Cordyline, Cyperus, Dieffenbachia, Dracaena, Fatshedera, Fatsia, Ferns, Ficus,

(Below)
Setcreasea purpurea, the Purple Heart, has narrow, elongated leaves of rosy-purple

(Bottom)
A young plant of *Schefflera actinophylla* which rapidly makes an elegant specimen house plant of some size

Fittonia, Hedera (plain-leaved vars.), Hoya, Maranta, Monstera, Palms, Philodendron, Rhoicissus, Sansevieria, Schefflera, Scindapsus, Schlumbergera, Spathiphyllum, Syngonium, Tradescantia, Zebrina.

Plants for cool rooms (but keep out frost) Acorus, Ampelopsis, Araucaria, Asparagus, Asplenium, many Cacti, Chlorophytum, *Cissus antarctica*, Citrus, Cyrtomium, Fatshedera, Fatsia, Grevillea, Hedera, Helxine, Jasminum, most Palms, Phyllitis, Pteris, *Saxifraga sarmentosa,* Schefflera, some Succulents, Tolmiea, Tradescantia, Zebrina.

Plants which will stand gas fires and similar fumes Aglaonema, Anthurium, Aspidistra, Bromeliads, Cacti, Chlorophytum, Clivia, Cyrtomium, Epiphyllum, Ficus, Hoya, Monstera, Palms, Peperomias, most Philodendrons, Platycerium, Sansevieria, Schefflera, Scindapsus, some Succulents, Syngonium, Tolmiea, Tradescantia, Zebrina.

Plants for bottle gardens Acorus, Aglaonema, *Begonia rex,* Bromeliads especially Cryptanthus, Calathea, *Cocos weddeliana,* Cordyline, Dracaena, Ferns, Maranta, Oplismenus, Pellionia, Peperomia, Pilea, Selaginella.

Permanent plants which flower Aechmea, Aeschynanthus, Anthurium, Aphelandra, some Begonias, Beloperone, Billbergia, Citrus, Clivia, Columnea, Epiphyllum, succulent Euphorbias, Hypocyrta, Impatiens, Jasminum, Rhipsalidopsis, Saintpaulia, Schlumbergera, Spathiphyllum, Vriesia.

cacti and succulents

what cacti and succulents are

Many families of plants which live in comparatively dry regions have evolved structures to withstand long periods of dryness. Such plants are scientifically known as xerophytes. Many such structures, though not all, can be classed under the heading of *succulence* – the provision of fleshy, water-retaining tissue, often protected in some way from the scorching effect of the sun. Cacti are perhaps the most obvious example of plants exhibiting this form of adaptation but, in fact, they compose only one of the many plant families which have succulent members.

Water requirements

Even the most highly specialised succulent plant requires some water, and no plant can live in completely arid desert. Some do live, nevertheless, in regions where the annual rainfall is as little as 3 or 4 in., and may be restricted to a single month. This, however, is exceptional, and night temperatures, which may fall to almost freezing-point, provoke heavy dew, which plays a considerable part in the life of such plants. In many regions where succulents grow, a fairly heavy rainfall is concentrated into a few weeks, while during the rest of the year little or no rain falls. But it must not be thought that succulent plants inhabit only semi-desert regions. Some of the *Cactaceae*, for instance, live as epiphytes – that is, perched on trees or rocks – in the tropical rain-forests of South America; and many of the others live in the African scrub and jungle.

The conditions in high mountains are basically similar to those in deserts, due to almost equally restricted rainfall, drying winds and, often, very limited soil. In winter the ground may be frozen and water is withheld from the plants. The hardy succulents, such as sedums and sempervivums, some of which are native to Britain, have been evolved in such conditions.

The grower of succulents does not usually include the hardy kinds; but this is a rather arbitrary outlook, for hardiness is relative, and some cacti which live on the high plateaux of Mexico, or in the Andes, may be covered in snow during the winter. That they and the other hardy succulents survive in the cold is due to their being dry at these times.

Heat and humidity

Some of the South African succulents will withstand a soil surface temperature of 60°C. (140°F.) and a relative air humidity as low as 10 per cent. Those species that live in scrub or forest are obviously accustomed to greater atmospheric humidity.

Water retention

The structural mechanisms developed to deal with severe drought conditions are varied and ingenious. They must clearly be devoted (1) to absorbing water quickly when it is available, via an extensive root-system, and (2) to reducing water loss (transpiration) to the minimum. In this way the maximum water is retained in the tissues – sometimes as much as 95 per cent. of the plant's volume is water.

In forms with leaves, these are almost always protected in some way against the full force of the sun. Often only a thin layer of cells is left to carry out photosynthesis, by which (together with minerals from the soil) the plant's food supply is produced: the rest of the tissue consists of water-storage cells. The outer skin is usually thick, often coated with wax or with white hairs, which act as an insulating medium.

The rosette arrangement of leaves is common, since it permits an extensive photosynthesising surface in the minimum space.

More often the leaves tend to diminish in number and size, and to become cylindrical or globular in shape, which reduces the area of

(Above)
The tongue-like, fleshy leaves of *Glottiphyllum arrectum* demonstrate the compact, water-retentive growth of succulents growing in fairly arid conditions

(Above right)
A compressed rosette of leaves, illustrated here by *Aeonium tabulaeforme*, is a further example of adaptation to climatic conditions

(Right)
The spines, which cover the surface of this cactus, *Echinocereus baileyi*, help to insulate the plant and may also act as reflectors in bright sunlight

transipration in relation to volume. They may be closely pressed to the stem, or in extreme examples the stem is dispensed with and the plant becomes a single, more or less globular body. The leaves may wither and shrink in the dry period, when no growth occurs at all.

Some of these 'plant-bodies' grow so that only the round, flattish top is exposed to the sun. In some curious examples a 'window' is formed at the top which reduces the power of the sun's rays but allows sufficient to reach the chlorophyll layer deep inside the plant-body.

This is one extreme: the other is the more or less complete absence of leaves. Most of the cacti are leafless or bear leaves for only a short time, and some other succulents, for example the euphorbias, are similar. Such plants, known as stem succulents, are thick and fleshy, consisting almost entirely of water-storage cells, with a thin photosynthesising layer protected by a thick skin – a function of the leaves taken over by the stem. They are usually globular or columnar, shapes again which minimise the proportion of surface area to volume. Many stem succulents also shrink in the dry season, to plump out again at the first rains.

Of course the minimisation of surface area reduces photosynthesis as well as transpiration. Hence the growth of the most highly drought-adapted forms is slow.

Another group accepted as succulents includes plants with normal leaves but which have a swollen or bulbous stem above ground. Ordinary bulbous and tuberous plants, with their swollen parts below ground, are not regarded as succulents, though indeed they are often adaptations to at least a seasonal period of drought.

Flowering succulents

Many people only like cacti if they flower readily and at an early age. Here are some cactus genera which can be recommended,

though to obtain flowers they must be re-
potted regularly, watered properly and, in
most cases, given full sun. Good nurserymen
will advise on the best flowering species:

Chamaecereus sylvestrii, Echinopsis eyriesii,
most species of *Gymnocalycium, Lobivia,
Mammillaria, Notocactus, Parodia* and *Rebutia*.

Among epiphytic cacti which need a warmer,
moister atmosphere, and also do well in
rooms, are *Aporocactus, Epiphyllum* hybrids,
Rhipsalidopsis rosea and *Schlumbergera* spp.

Other succulents which give regular, showy
blooms are *Crassula falcata, Delosperma* spp.,
many *Echeveria* spp., *Euphorbia bojeri* and *E.
splendens, Kalanchoë blossfeldiana* and its
modern varieties, *Lampranthus* and other
shrubby *Mesembryanthemum* spp., *Oscularia*
spp., *Rochea coccinea,* and *Stapelia* spp.

Cristates

It is fairly common to find various garden
plants with a flattened or distorted stem. This
is usually due to fasciation, a phenomenon in
which the growing point of a stem divides and
multiplies abnormally. Fasciated succulents
are known as cristates.

Among succulents, especially cacti, this is
very common, and there are a large number of
cristate forms, which are sometimes beautiful
and always extraordinary. Some cristates
develop in one direction only, resulting in a
flat fan-like growth which in time becomes
convoluted, not unlike coral; in others a vast
number of tiny heads is produced, or sometimes the rib and tubercle formation becomes
entirely irregular. Examples of the latter two
are often referred to as monstrosities rather
than cristates. The Latin word *monstrosus* or
cristatus after the specific name indicates a
fasciated variety.

Cristate cacti are reproduced by grafting or,
if suitable, from cuttings; cristate succulents
other than cacti are increased by cuttings.
Seed seldom reproduces cristation.

(Opposite page top)
Ferocactus latispinus, a cactus, showing white,
cushion-like areoles with spines (left); *Aloe ferox*,
a succulent, with prickly points on the leaves
(right)

(Opposite page bottom)
A plant of *Coryphantha erecta* showing the
tubercles, each of which is tipped by a spine-
bearing areole

(Below)
The cristate forms of the succulents have a
certain fascination. *Cereus peruvianus monstrosus* is illustrated

the families of succulents

When referring to succulents many people speak rather of 'cacti' and include in that name the other groups – if, indeed, they realise that there are other groups. Now, the cacti are members of the family *Cactaceae*; it is certainly an important one, but it is only one of the families with succulent members.

It is, of course, the flowers that reveal the family, the flower being the only part of the plant which retains its basic structure whatever adaptations the leaves and stems may have made. There are members of other families which are almost indistinguishable from cacti to the casual eye, but the flowers are entirely different when examined carefully.

The *Cactaceae* are almost exclusively natives of America. There are a few other succulents in America, but on the whole the other groups are African. The close resemblance of some American and some African species is a nice example of what is known scientifically as parallel evolution – the modification of members of unrelated families into similar forms and structures to meet a similar set of climatic conditions.

There is a certain amount of nomenclatural confusion among the genera. In the most important families, the *Cactaceae* and *Aizoaceae*, the first plants of each to be found were given the names, respectively, of *Cactus* and *Mesembryanthemum*. As more and more different plants were discovered, however, it soon became plain that these names were insufficient to classify the families. For it must be remembered that names are not given merely for identification; if that were so all the *Cactaceae* might, indeed, be regarded as different species of a genus *Cactus*.

The names are also a guide to classification. Thus the families have been gradually divided into more and more genera as the botanists find details which will segregate them, and botanists differ in their ideas of what generic and specific names also may be accepted. This accounts for the various names under which some plants may be found. I have kept synonyms to the minimum, but these facts should be remembered if you see a familiar plant under another name.

In the following pages are outlined the main characteristics of the families with succulent members which are included in this book.

The Cactaceae

A family almost entirely succulent and usually leafless. The more primitive and unadapted members are those which are least succulent and may have leaves.

The cushion-like areoles are unique to the cacti. These may be covered in wool or hair, or small bristles called glochids, and may sprout spines. It is at the areoles that the flowers usually appear; in *Mammillaria*, however, they do so between the tubercles. The flowers

(Top)
Opuntia compressa, a member of the *Opuntieae*, one of the tribes of the *Cactaceae*, is typical of the Prickly Pears, which have flat, leaf-like 'pads', although some opuntias have cylindrical stems

(Bottom)
Epiphyllum ackermannii is representative of the epiphytic plants classed within the *Cereeae*. An epiphyte is a plant which, in the wild, grows on another without being in any way a parasite

(Top)
Another member of the *Cereeae*, *Coryphantha vivipara* has a typical 'cactus' appearance. The spines are large and sprout from the cushion-like areoles at the top of the tubercles

(Bottom)
The smaller-spined *Echinocereus subinermis* is a member of a genus of easily grown plants notable for their very beautiful flowers

have a large, indeterminate number of petals and stamens; there is generally no clear distinction between petals and sepals. The ovary is 'inferior', i.e. below every other part of the flower. The flowers are often large, showy and bright. The fruit is a single-celled berry, frequently fleshy but sometimes dry, usually brightly coloured, with many seeds.

The *Cactaceae* are divided into three tribes, as follows.

The Pereskieae A small group of primitive cacti which are hardly succulent at all. They are mainly twiggy bushes or sub-shrubs, bearing spines and glossy leaves. The main genus is *Pereskia*, and most of the species are Mexican in origin.

The Opuntieae An extensive tribe containing the well-known Prickly Pears. Botanically they are separated from other cacti by the presence of glochids in the areoles – fine, barbed bristles which can be very irritating if they enter the skin. Some have awl-shaped leaves which are often only carried for a short time, and the stems are divided into more or less regular, often flattened joints. The main genus, *Opuntia*, contains many species, is spread from Canada to Cape Horn, and has been naturalised in the Mediterranean area, Australia and elsewhere.

The Cereeae This tribe contains the majority of cacti, and its members are found from Canada to Patagonia. Owing to its size, it is much subdivided.

The Aizoaceae

This is a family (sometimes called *Ficoidaceae* or *Mesembryanthemaceae*) exclusively composed of succulents, from S. and S.W. Africa. The species used to be classed under the single genus *Mesembryanthemum*, but this has been greatly divided up, and the name now only refers to a few annual and biennial species which make good bedding plants.

The flowers of the *Aizoaceae* are bi-sexual, with either many petals or none, 4 or 5 sepals, 4, 5 or many stamens, and an ovary of 2 or more cells giving rise to a capsular fruit. Flowers are large and bright in a wide range of colours, and superficially resemble daisies.

The plants exhibit gradations of form according to the amount of specialisation imposed by the habitat. First there are shrubby, more or less woody plants, with leaves arranged in well-spaced opposite pairs, one pair at right angles to the next. These are usually easy to grow, flower freely and are often used in gardens. They include species of *Carpobrotus*, *Delosperma*, *Drosanthemum*, *Lampranthus* and *Oscularia*.

Then there are plants with fairly long stems but much fleshier leaves, more closely packed on the stems. These merge into the really fleshy forms, where the stems are almost or entirely absent, often with only a few pairs of leaves, still in the cruciate pattern which is, in such forms, much more marked, though sometimes obscured by crowding. Among the genera here are *Argyroderma*, *Cheiridopsis*, *Faucaria*, *Gibbaeum*, *Glottiphyllum*, *Pleiospilos* and *Stomatium*.

The next stage comes when these leaves are reduced to two; there are forms in which the leaves are partly joined, and these lead into those in which the leaves have been converted into a single solid mass or plant-body. The division between the pair is sometimes marked by a groove or slit, may be reduced to a small aperture or may have disappeared. Notable genera in this group are *Conophytum*, *Lithops* and *Ophthalmophyllum*.

These are most surprising when they produce their flowers, which are often bigger than the bodies themselves. At other times many of these succulents are very difficult to see, since their shape and colouring are so similar to surrounding stones. Their nickname is 'living stones' or 'stone mimics'.

continued on page 76

(Below)
This collection of succulents shows some of the many different forms in existence and includes examples of grafted and cristate cacti

The plants illustrated on these two pages are all members of the *Crassulaceae* and show the diversity of form existing within this family

(Top)
Echeveria pulvinata

(Bottom)
Pachyphytum amethystinum

(Top)
.A selection of forms from the very variable genus *Crassula*; left, *C. arborescens*; centre, *C. lycopo-dioides*; and right, *C. rupestris*

(Bottom)
Sedum guatamalense

(Right)
Sedum morganianum

Apart from these are the 'window plants', (see page 68), for example *Fenestraria,* which might be taken for plant-bodies, but which are in fact groups of cylindrical leaves arising from one stem.

Lastly there is a group of annuals, small branching plants, two of which, *Dorotheanthus* and *Mesembryanthemum crystallinum,* are commonly treated as half-hardy annuals and can be very showy.

The Crassulaceae

This next-largest family of succulent plants includes many hardy species. The leaves are usually either in opposite pairs at right angles, in rosettes or arranged spirally up the stem. The flowers, usually carried in a cluster, are bi-sexual and regular, with 4 or 5 petals and the same number of sepals.

The names of the genera have been very much muddled, and one species may have three or four generic synonyms. One group is centred on the hardy *Sempervivum,* and includes the tender *Aeonium* and *Greenovia. Sedum,* the stonecrops, is another genus which is fairly clearly defined.

The other important genera are *Adromischus, Bryophyllum, Cotyledon, Crassula, Echeveria, Kalanchoë, Pachyphytum* and *Rochea.*

Many of these are very attractive, and almost all are easy to grow, apart from some very specialised desert crassulas. They are widely distributed in America, Africa and to a lesser extent Asia, and show succulent forms provoked not only by heat and drought but by cold and drought.

The Asclepiadaceae

This family is far from exclusively succulent. The succulent genera are on the whole African, and there are some from India and the East Indies. Most of them are leafless and superficially cactus-like, the genus *Stapelia* being the representative example.

The *Asclepiadaceae* have bizarre flowers, reaching the height of oddity in *Ceropegia.* Botanically they are regular; the anthers are joined to the stigma; and the seeds, which are produced in a pair of long horn-like or pod-like follicles, are usually tufted with hair, a dispersal device.

The Compositae

It would be surprising if the largest of all plant families had not produced some succulent forms. The huge genus *Senecio,* which includes our native ragwort and groundsel, contains a number of diverse succulent forms exhibiting different stages of adaptation to drought. This genus now includes *Kleinia* which contains species equally diverse in form. All have typical composite flowers, disconcertingly like those of groundsel. Most of the species come from South and South-west Africa; others from other parts of Africa and from the East Indies.

The Euphorbiaceae

One of the most extensive single genera, *Euphorbia* contains a large number of succulent forms, mostly very cactus-like, but distinguishable partly by the entirely dissimilar flowers and by usually having milky juice. The genus displays the most astonishing diversity of form and adaptation. Some species are woody or herbaceous with normal leaves, while others have reduced leaves, and stems which are succulent and cactiform. The flowers are of two sexes, usually carried in cyathia, in which a petal-less female flower is surrounded by brighter petal-like structures. Sometimes the male and female flowers are carried on separate plants. Very often leaves are absent or primitive.

The succulent euphorbias occur in South and North Africa, Madagascar, Canary Islands, Arabia, E. Indies, a few in America, and are naturalised elsewhere.

The Liliaceae

The succulent *Liliaceae* are mainly rosette plants, the leaves being often, as in *Aloe* – one of the most widely spread African succulents – held at the end of a woody stem. Other genera include *Apicra, Gasteria* (in which the leaves are carried in two rows) and *Haworthia,* which contains a variety of small rosette plants including several 'window' plants.

The flowers of these plants are like trumpet lilies in miniature, carried on long stems, but often insignificant.

Less important families

Among the other families which have a few succulent species – perhaps 35 all told – the following are mentioned in this book. Representatives of the families not described are either rare in nature, not in commerce, or very difficult to cultivate.

Agavaceae Includes the extensive American genus *Agave,* formerly placed in *Amaryllidaceae.* This genus has been naturalised also in Europe and Africa.

Geraniaceae The common pelargoniums so much used for bedding in some countries are themselves more or less fleshy; and there are several really succulent members of this genus from arid regions of South and South-west Africa, as well as the entirely leafless, greatly drought-resisting *Sarcocaulon* (rarely grown), from the same area.

Portulacaceae This family, represented in Britain by purslane and other weedy plants, is naturally fleshy, and it is difficult to draw the line as to which are succulents and which are not. One species, the Brazilian *Portulaca grandiflora,* is familiar as the parent of a race of showy half-hardy annuals.

Vitaceae The vine family is represented by a number of African species of *Cissus* (a genus mostly of climbers) with greatly swollen stems from which, in the growing season, large fleshy leaves are produced.

(Top)
A selection of the species found in *Stapelia*. This curious genus is typical of the succulent members of the *Asclepiadaceae*

(Bottom)
A group of species of *Conophytum* —one of the most highly adapted genera of the *Aizoaceae*. The leaves are reduced to a single mass or plant-body which varies in size and shape

cultivation in greenhouse and home

Despite all the differences of family and habitat, most succulent plants can be grown in similar soil, temperature and air conditions: they are nothing if not adaptable. To get the best results, with steady growth and regular flowering, the needs of some groups must be properly studied; but few succulents can be killed if the basic essentials are followed.

In the winter especially, the main difference to natural conditions is lack of light. Fortunately, in many cases these plants adjust themselves readily to our seasons, and our winter becomes their resting period. At this time, freedom from frost and considerable if not total reduction of watering are all that is necessary. The imitation of the resting period is the most important aspect of cultivation indoors. Plants which will not rest in the winter need great care.

The greenhouse

A greenhouse is the best place in which to grow succulents. It should be in a sunny position and should permit the entry of the maximum amount of light. For this reason large panes are best. Good ventilation is equally essential, for even our relatively weak sun may damage succulents if they are in a stuffy, moist atmosphere; also soft growth may result, liable to rotting in winter. Thus a wide span is desirable, with side, roof and, if possible, wall ventilators.

These are ideal requirements: almost any greenhouse will do. If the house is very small, however, ventilation becomes even more important, as it is so easy for conditions to become stuffy, and also for pots to dry out.

Attention should be paid to the floor, so that surplus water drains away freely. A concrete floor, with slight slope into a drainage channel and drain, is ideal.

For most plants staging at about waist height is adequate. The usual wooden slats will do, but a solid base on which a layer of small gravel or coarse grit is spread is better, and it is useful to have a section of staging which can be built up to form a bed into which pots can be plunged. This is particularly so with the smaller *Aizoaceae*, as explained later. High shelves close to the glass are useful for ripening such plants in their resting period, and also to accommodate plants which hang or trail. Water must be able to drain away from solid staging or beds.

If very large specimens are in question, they are best set either in pots or planted direct in a prepared bed at ground level.

It is not advisable to mix succulents and other greenhouse plants, for the latter require far more atmospheric humidity, but it can be done if necessary.

(Right)
A selection of cacti and other succulents which can be grown in a small greenhouse

(Top)
Periodic repotting is essential to maintain plant vigour. The plant should be carefully knocked out of its pot, as shown

(Bottom)
As much of the old soil as possible is teased away from the roots; if necessary, a pointed stick can be a useful aid in removing compacted soil. Dead or broken roots should be cut back

(Top)
The plant is placed in a slightly larger pot so that the soil comes up to the original level. Fresh soil is trickled in round the roots

(Bottom)
The soil is firmed as it is added and the plant given a final firming to allow about a ½ in. space below the pot rim

Heating and ventilation

The greenhouse must have some provision for heating in winter, to maintain a minimum temperature of at least 4° C. (40° F.). Temperatures below this are harmful to most succulents, and some prefer a higher winter temperature. It is simpler, perhaps, to keep such plants in a different house or at least well separated from others. Where lower winter temperatures are desirable as with some cacti which flower less freely, if not kept cold at this season, this is indicated in the alphabetical list of succulent genera.

For heating a small house the common paraffin heater may be used, with the usual care to prevent fumes, which may damage plants. Hot-water pipes heated by a boiler are standard in many houses, and are quite efficient but tedious to maintain. Electric tubular heating, controlled by a thermostat, is the ideal. It is relatively cheap to instal and at 4 – 8° C. (40 – 47° F.) reasonably cheap to run; the thermostat prevents waste, often difficult to achieve with boilers, and there is little maintenance or worry involved.

Succulents always like fresh air, and should be given as much as possible, winter and summer, as long as the weather is suitable. In winter, ventilators should be opened by day as long as the required temperature is maintained, and there is no fog or mist. Draughts must be avoided: therefore those ventilators away from the wind must be opened – another reason for having plenty of them.

As spring progresses, there will be less need to heat the house; but watch must be kept for sudden cold spells and frosty nights, particularly if a previous warm spell has started the plants into growth. It is here that an automatic heating system scores.

In warm weather the main thing to watch is ventilation. On hot, still days all the vents can be opened. If it is windy those on the windward side are closed, for even in summer

(Below)
A prickly plant can be handled more easily if a piece of folded paper is passed around the stem. This can be used to hold the plant throughout the potting operation

draughts should be avoided. Movement of air is necessary though, especially if the weather is damp and the air moist. In a variable climate some closing of vents at night is advisable to guard against a change of wind direction or driving rain.

The mechanisms that open and close ventilators as the temperature fluctuates are valuable, especially if the house has to be left unattended.

Shading

Most succulents do not require much shading, though under glass, in very bright weather with no air movement, yellowing or scorching may occur if temperatures go over 27° C. (80° F.). All highly adapted forms need maximum sunlight at all times, and the glass must be kept clean to ensure this. Only a few must be shaded; they include the epiphytic cacti. Where a plant requires shading, this is stated in the list of succulent genera.

The best means of shading such plants is a thin film of whitewash with a very little linseed oil, on the outside of the glass; commercial materials are too thick.

When sunlight is weak and infrequent in winter, as much as possible must reach our plants. Therefore the glass should be well washed in autumn, and this should be repeated as and when necessary, particularly in towns where grime soon films the glass.

Staging

As with any kind of pot plant, succulents should be placed on the staging so that they are graded in size from front to back, ensuring that they all receive equal amounts of light and that they are easily reached.

A small shelf at the back of the staging may be useful for display if the collection consists mostly of little plants, and also to place hanging-type plants on. Alternatively, such plants can be placed on an inverted pot.

Some growers bury their pots up to the rims in a deep bed of grit or gravel. This is, in fact, advisable with the small *Aizoaceae* and other tricky plants, since the bed is watered, not the pots, and the dangers of direct watering are avoided. The roots emerge from the drainage holes and seek moisture in the bed of grit. Of course, plants with different resting periods must be kept well apart.

This is admirable if one does not want to take the plants to shows, and if one has the patience to leave a semi-permanent arrangement alone. It permits a more naturalistic display, and the 'stone-imitating' plants, for instance, can be grouped with similar stones to demonstrate their camouflage. Small grit is placed over the whole surface, hiding the pot rims and giving a natural-looking finish.

Direct planting into the soil cannot be recommended unless the arrangement is to be well-nigh permanent.

Soil mixtures

The adaptable succulents can be grown in almost any sort of soil so long as it is porous and properly drained; but a well-balanced mixture will, other things being equal, give better results – steady growth, regular flowering, freedom from disease.

Though a large number of recipes can be found in older books, modern experience shows that John Innes Potting Compost No. 1 is as good for most succulents as it is for other plants, preferably adapted by adding 1 part of some gritty material – coarse sand, road grit, small brick or pot chips, or vermiculite – to every 4 parts made-up compost. Ready-mixed composts modified in this way can be bought. Really strong-growing plants such as aloes, agaves, opuntias, cereus, can go into John Innes No. 2 or No. 3 mixtures, which contain more fertiliser.

South African succulents, such as lithops, conophytum etc., need more sandy compost

(Top)
Lampranthus amoenus, an attractive species which can be grown out of doors as a half-hardy perennial, being bedded out for summer flowering and returned to frost-free conditions in winter

(Bottom)
The Livingstone Daisy, popularly sold as *Mesembryanthemum criniflorum*, is a delightful half-hardy annual for summer display

without fertiliser: a suitable mix is 2 parts loam, 2 parts coarse sand and 1 part peat. Jungle cacti – epiphyllum, schlumbergera etc. – like much richer compost, say 2 parts loam, 1 part coarse sand, and 1 part leafmould, spent mushroom compost, or peat, adding 3 oz. hoof and horn meal, 3 oz. superphosphate and $1\frac{1}{2}$ oz. sulphate of potash per bushel.

If making up your own compost, avoid any organic material that is still decomposing, like insufficiently rotted manure or compost. Loam should be medium to heavy, without too much fibre – except for the jungle cacti – and should if possible be sterilised. Sand should be really coarse, with only a small proportion of particles below $\frac{1}{16}$ in. Small gravel or stone chips can be added, as well as crushed bricks from $\frac{1}{4} - \frac{3}{4}$ in. in size.

Potting

Succulents need repotting like any other plants, and those that grow rapidly will fill a pot with roots in a year. The most frequent causes of collapse are allowing plants to become so root-bound that there is insufficient food in the soil, and clogged drainage, both of which are averted by regular repotting.

As for any plant, pots and crocks should be clean and sterile. The best time to repot most cacti is between March and May; other plants as soon as signs of renewed growth are seen, and preferably when the outside temperature is at least 13° C. (55° F.). Succulents *can* be repotted at any time, so long as there is active growth, and if a plant is doing badly the first thing to do is to look at the roots.

Young and vigorous plants may need annual potting, and others are best repotted every two or three years. Slow growers with poor root systems may be left longer. Before repotting, the soil should be fairly dry. With some plants the orthodox method of turning out of the pot may be used, holding the stem in one hand, the pot upside down and tapping

the rim on the edge of the bench or staging. As so many succulents are brittle, it may be safer to push the root ball up with a finger or stick through the drainage hole. Holding the plant is not always easy: small, soft plants must be held very gently, and with spiny ones leather gloves should be worn or the stem held in a pair of padded tongs. Alternatively, a strip of newspaper, folded over and over and passed round the plant, is handy.

Once the plant is out of its pot, some of the old soil can be picked away, using a pointed stick if necessary, and a look-out kept for various pests (see page 97). Be careful not to pull away too many of the fine root-hairs. Dead or broken roots should be cut back to living tissue with a razor-blade or very sharp knife. Cut surfaces are best dusted with sulphur or charcoal dust. Any decay on the plant should be dealt with when repotting; also clean off dead leaves, dry skin, etc.

The new pot should accommodate the roots easily, with a little room to spare. If the plant is large but the roots are limited, a shallow pan is desirable, or the result may be top-heavy. Conversely, a plant with a long tap-root, like many cacti, needs a long narrow pot.

Crocks should cover the hole, but a deep layer is not usually necessary. A layer of stone chips can be placed over this. There is no need to overdo the drainage: all that is required is to ensure that excess water should be able to run out freely, without any danger of keeping the soil wet and stagnant.

The plant should be replaced so that the soil comes up to the original level. Hold it in position and let the fresh soil trickle in round the roots, tapping the pot on the bench to shake it down, and if necessary pushing the soil in with a stick. The soil should be firm but not rammed down, and come up to about $\frac{1}{2}$ in. below the pot rim. A layer of small stone chips on the surface will prevent the soil caking or becoming compressed.

Plants in bowls

The average fancier of succulent plants will keep his plants in separate pots, which allows full individual control of watering. He will, indeed, turn up his nose at plants kept in bowls. But for the person with only a few plants, particularly if they are kept in a living-room, bowl arrangement is both convenient and far more decorative than a number of pots.

Obviously, only plants with similar requirements should be grown together. It is no use growing *Aizoaceae* which have a winter growing period together with cacti which rest at that time. But the majority of popular succulents can be treated alike.

It is best to use wide, shallow bowls with drainage holes, and earthenware seed-pans are ideal. If these are used, planting and cultivation are the same as for plants in separate pots. However, such bowls are seldom decorative, and if kept in a room need a plate below them to prevent water pouring

(Below)
Many succulents have extensive roots. The pot should be large enough to hold these while allowing room for a layer of crocks and stone chips to ensure drainage

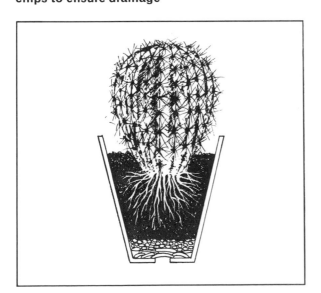

out on to the furniture. It is perfectly possible to keep succulents in bowls without drainage, and in glazed bowls at that; I myself kept a considerable number in bowls for many years. Designs can be made including small rocks, and a layer of stone chippings on the compost can be added as a final touch.

If undrained bowls are used, it is essential to have a deep layer of small crocks, so that if surplus water collects it is well away from the soil; it is equally important to keep watering to a minimum to prevent too much water collecting, especially in winter. Even so, it is surprising how much water such bowls can receive, and how quickly it will evaporate in warm weather. The bowls are usually shallow, and the deep layer of crocks means a relatively thin layer of soil. Under these conditions the plants may not grow very fast, but obviously it is undesirable for plants in containers of this kind to grow too large. Small plants, seedlings or cuttings, such as are sold by florists, are ideal for bowls. Give them reasonable room, and repot every year to make sure that the roots – which will tend to spread sideways – do not become starved or tangled together.

Watering

Most succulent plants, when in full growth, take as much water as any pot plant, but since they are constructed to exist with little, it is better to under-water than to kill the roots by over-watering.

At the beginning of the growing period water is given occasionally, and gradually increased as required. As with ordinary plants, watering is only necessary when the soil begins to dry out after the previous application. The soil on the surface may look dry, but to make sure it is best to scrape down a little way or, when experience is gained, to judge by tapping or lifting the pot.

With almost all cacti and most of the other succulents whose growing period coincides with our summer, three or more waterings a week may be needed in hot weather. Obviously, plants in small pots, and those with vigorous root systems, will need a lot of water.

Towards the end of the growing period – about mid-September for the average succulent – watering is gradually curtailed; this helps ripening. Cacti may shrivel a little at this time, but this is quite natural. In the resting period one light watering a week is ample, and if the conditions are on the cold side, much less may suffice. In winter only enough water should be given to prevent the soil from drying out completely. At this time especially, *if in doubt do not water*: the roots are largely inactive. Never splash water about: this may lead to condensation on the plants if the temperature falls.

Where succulents have well defined rest periods these must be carefully observed. Not until the first signs of new growth are clearly visible should watering begin; and as soon as the plant begins to shrivel watering should be

sharply restricted, and with many plants, as specified in the alphabetical list of genera, entirely stopped. Otherwise rotting often follows, or at least flowering may be prevented. Seedlings may, however, usually be watered sparingly in their first resting period. With these plants it is always best to be cautious about quantities. The method of watering grit in which pots are buried is ideal (see page 83 and illustration below left).

It is wise to avoid pouring water on to plants; it may possibly cause rotting and I have seen drops of water acting as lenses in hot sun and causing scorch marks. Some growers in warm climates syringe their plants lightly in the early evening to simulate the desert dew. This may be carried out in very hot weather, but it is rarely necessary in cooler climates and can easily be overdone. An occasional spray, with water to which a little soft soap has been added, is useful to clean the plants, especially in the sooty, acid-laden air of towns or in dusty rooms. On such occasions the plant should be sprayed again with clear water, and then shaken to avoid water lodging in any crevice. Woolly cacti may be 'shampooed' with a soft brush dipped in soapy water, and succulents with stiff leaves, such as agaves

(Below)
Sinking pots of succulents in grit in a container gives an effective control of growth (left); when planting direct into an undrained bowl, it is important to use a deep layer of crocks (right)

and aloes, may be gently washed with a soft rag dipped in soapy water and then cleaned off with clear water; but avoid this with plants having a 'bloom' on the leaves.

Keeping succulents in rooms

It is quite easy to cultivate succulents in rooms, except the highly adapted forms. The main requirement is sunlight, and therefore a southerly aspect is best, placing the plants as near the window as possible.

A collection of pots can be accommodated in earthenware pans, and if these are filled up with coarse sand or gravel, a generous layer being left below the pots, they will look more attractive and will not dry out too quickly. This applies particularly to the very small plants often sold by florists. Alternatively,

(Below)
In a room, a collection of succulents can be attractively grouped together in a bowl to create a long-lasting decoration

they can be planted direct into pans or bowls (see page 85). Containers of window-box shape can also be used.

The window-sill is the best place for them, but it is often too narrow. However, a wide wooden board, supported on angle brackets, may be fixed to the sill, or if this is undesirable, legs may be fitted, either to make a removable table-like support or so that one side rests on the existing sill. Such a board may be treated just like the staging in a greenhouse and, if equipped with upright sides, may be filled up with grit.

During the summer, air is as important as sun. At least the windows should be opened at all opportunities; if possible, the plants should be placed outside. If the window-ledge is not wide enough, some sort of board, tray or even a projecting frame with glass sides and removable lid can be fixed outside, making sure the supports are strong enough. The lid is useful in heavy rain.

With all these adjuncts, a waterproof lining, such as zinc, may be added to prevent damage to the wood from water dripping through.

Watering follows the rules already laid down. If the room is heated in winter, the pots will dry out rapidly and should be watered more often. But be very cautious, as over-watering in poor light conditions leads to soft growth which rots all too readily. It is really best to withdraw the plants to a room where the temperature is fairly constant and cool and the need for water is reduced.

In winter, guard against frost and draughts. Plants on window-sills may have to be removed, or protected with paper or curtains, if it is very cold outside. Do not draw curtains so as to leave plants overnight between them and the window: if it is freezing outside the plants will certainly suffer.

Plants on a window-sill or ledge should be turned periodically so that each side receives an equal amount of light.

propagation of succulents

From seed

Succulents are raised from seed as easily as most tropical plants, but some grow very slowly from seedlings, especially certain cacti. Seed of many species is generally available but may often be hybrid.

A mixture of sterilised soil, sand and peat may be used for seed sowing, or the John Innes Seed Compost is suitable.

Half-pots, small pans or seed-boxes are suitable containers. They should be very well crocked. The seed is often extremely small, and if dust-like should not be covered; otherwise a very light sifting of fine sand is adequate; large seeds may be lightly pressed in. Seeds should be well spaced. Some growers place a 'one-stone' layer of coarse sand or grit on top which helps to avoid drying and caking of the soil surface. The receptacle should be soaked by immersing up to the edge: top watering would disturb the seed. A sprinkling of Cheshunt compound through a very fine spray will help to avoid damping-off disease and the growth of algae.

These seeds need a temperature of 21° C. (70° F.) to germinate well, and a propagating case is the ideal place to germinate them. If this is impossible, a warm situation must be found and the container covered with a sheet of glass (turn over daily to avoid condensation), and preferably placed in a box containing damp peat to supply adequate moisture.

If the bottom heat is available, sowing can be done in February or March: if not, wait until April or May. When germination begins air must be adequate or damping-off will occur. At this moment, too, adequate light is essential or the seedlings will be weak and spindly, but keep them out of direct sunlight. Some seedlings appear after a few days; some take up to a month, and some much longer, especially if the seed is not fresh. Hence the advisability of sowing each kind in a separate receptacle. Seeds should remain viable for at least two years.

Quick-growing seedlings may be pricked out (i.e. replanted in other receptacles) soon after germination; but most seedlings grow so slowly at first that it is best to sow very thinly and leave the little plants in their pans for some months, until they are at least $\frac{1}{2}$ in. in diameter or 1 in. tall, according to shape. A miniature two-pronged fork made from a piece of thin wood is useful for lifting seedlings. Care should be taken not to damage the fine roots when lifting them, and the seedlings should not be firmed too hard into the new soil.

Small seedlings should be moved into the John Innes Seed Compost; larger ones into the adult compost already described (see page 83). Several seedlings can be placed in one pan or individual small pots can be used, but these need watching against the possibility of their drying out in hot conditions.

Watering must be carefully attended to both before and after germination. The boxes, pans or pots should never become quite dry. Bottom watering is best until the plants are fairly large. The resting season should not, normally, be observed until the second year, when the plants become adults.

Great care must be taken to keep away slugs, snails and woodlice, and to make sure of preventing damping-off water monthly with Cheshunt compound. Protection from scorching sun is also necessary.

By cuttings

Most succulents are readily increased by cuttings. Apart from mere multiplication of specimens, it is often possible to improve the shape of a weak or distorted plant by taking cuttings from it, for the removal of a part often promotes fresh growth; alternatively, the old plant can be replaced by the better-grown youngster. But the mere pleasure of rooting new plants so easily should not allow one to spoil a well-shaped plant, particularly if it is a cactus with a number of offsets attractively growing around it. Some people think it necessary to remove such offsets; but this is not so.

(Above left)
The mammillarias are a fascinating and varied genus. *M. elongata* shows the typical formation of tubercles, areoles and spines

(Left)
The enchanting star-like flowers of *Mammillaria geulzowiana* makes this one of the many species which are well worth growing

(Right)
Propagation by cuttings and offsets: the black line shows position of cut. 1-4 various cacti; 5. *Opuntia* with pads; 6. *Mammillaria* (tubercles); 7. branching cactus or *Euphorbia*; 8. *Zygocactus*; 9. other jointed plants; 10. offset on rosette plant; 11. branching rosette plant, e.g. *Aeonium*; 12. branching *Crassulaceae*; leaves can often be used; 13. branching shrubby *Mesembryanthemum*; 14. *Bryophyllum* (adventitious buds); 15. *Lithops* type; divide clump or take cutting

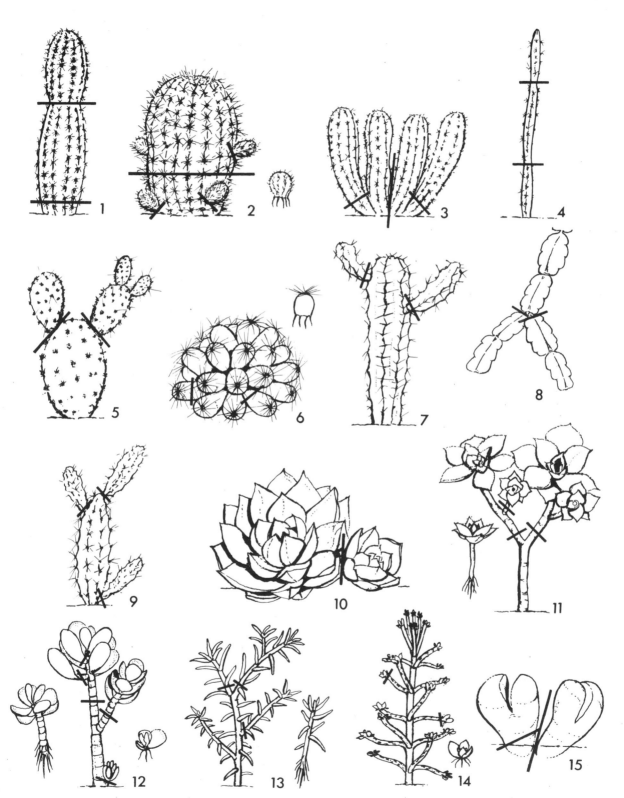

The parts of a plant which can be used vary according to the family (see line drawing on page 91). Most cacti produce young plantlets or offsets; or branches can be used. With opuntias the pads, and with epiphyllums and other leaf-like cacti the stem-segments, are used. Wherever a stem is jointed, not less than one joint should be used. Columnar cacti can be beheaded and the top pieces rooted; those with long thin stems are cut up into suitable lengths. Clump-forming cacti can be separated. The tubercles of mammillarias and similar genera can be cut off and rooted, though usually enough offsets are produced.

Cactus-like succulents, such as many euphorbias and *Stapelia* and its relations, are treated in the same way, separating branches or offsets or beheading columnar stems. The latter method obviously ruins the parent plant, and is usually only resorted to when the base is damaged or has become woody, or the roots have decayed.

Agaves, aloes, haworthias, gasterias, etc., produce easily removed offsets. Many kinds of *Bryophyllum* produce adventitious buds on the leaves, which make roots while still on the parent. Almost all succulents can be increased by stem cuttings, and most *Crassulaceae* by leaves as well. These are usually very easily detached, and if pushed into sandy compost, or even laid on its surface, root and produce new leaves around the base. Leaves of *Aloe* and *Haworthia* will also root. In fact, many succulents often put out roots if simply left lying in the air.

The *Aizoaceae* can be increased by stem cuttings; leaves will not root. The shrubby species root readily, but the fleshy ones are more difficult. Each pair of leaves, or plant-body in the highly succulent forms, can be treated as a cutting; the base of the plant must be undamaged.

Cuttings can be taken at any time, but late spring to high summer is best; at other times there is the danger of rotting due to damp and cold. Bottom heat is helpful but not essential. If the pots or boxes can be watered from the bottom so much the better. Avoid a close atmosphere, which may provoke basal decay. It is advisable to provide shade from full sun.

For rooting, the usual potting compost, with some extra grit, can be used, but pure *coarse* sand, or a mixture of sand and peat, is better; vermiculite, which holds moisture like the peat mixture, promotes very quick rooting. With all these the plants need to be potted up fairly soon after rooting, as no food is present. Perhaps the best method is to place the cuttings in a layer of coarse sand or vermiculite over the potting mixture.

The most important thing when taking cuttings of these plants is to dry them well. After making the cut, with a sharp knife or razor-blade, the cuttings must be left in a warm, dry place until a callus, or skin, has formed over the cut surface. With very fleshy cacti and some genera of the *Aizoaceae*, a period of several weeks may be needed. Never insert a cutting until the cut is well and truly dried, nor overwater the rooting material. The pieces to be rooted should not be pushed in at all deeply.

Grafting

Most cacti can be grafted on to other cacti. I have never heard of grafting practised on other kinds of succulent, but it is presumably feasible in some instances.

There are occasions when grafting helps a weakly or slow-growing cactus to grow more strongly, or quickly, or allows the cultivation of species which are impossible to grow on their own roots. Sometimes a hanging cactus is grafted to the top of a columnar form to produce a result like a weeping standard rose. Apart from these more or less necessary cases, I think grafted plants are ugly and unnecessary, though sometimes grotesque

(Top)
Succulents usually grow readily from seed; the container is crocked and a layer of stone chippings is added

(Bottom)
The container is filled with compost, which is firmed with the fingers and then levelled with a flat, smooth block of wood

(Top)
Seed is sown as thinly as possible, and all but the smallest should be covered with a light sifting of fine sand

(Bottom)
A thin covering of grit, or coarse sand, after sowing keeps the soil moist and helps to prevent algal growth

combinations may elicit a reluctant fascination.

The basis of cactus grafting is to make flat cuts which correspond on stock and scion, and to press them together immediately. Horizontal, ∨ or ∧-shaped cuts may be used. When the scion is a thin or flattened plant, such as *Aporocactus* or *Schlumbergera* respectively, a wedge graft is used; a narrow cleft should be cut in the stock, and the edges of the scion should be pared of the outer skin to provide sufficient cut surface.

Schlumbergera is sometimes grafted fanwise on to large *Opuntia* pads. Very thin round stems, such as of *Pereskia*, may be pushed into a hole in a large cactus. Various combinations will suggest themselves.

The two parts are generally pinned together, usually with an unbarbed cactus spine, which will not rust like a metal pin. Alternatively, twine is placed around the base of the pot and the graft, using paper or cotton-wool as padding if necessary. Weighted twine can also be used and avoids the need for making a knot.

Union should occur in a week or two. If the plants are pinned together, the spine should eventually be removed to avoid rotting; other fixing should be left for three weeks. In any case, great care should be taken to avoid jolting the union during the first three weeks. Nor should any water reach the point of union during this time, or rotting may occur. Otherwise conditions are the same as for normal plants.

Grafting should be done in summer when the day temperature is between 18 – 21° C. (65 – 70° F.), and when the atmosphere is dry. Full ventilation should be given to promote air circulation.

(Left)
Euphorbia is a large genus including a number of very different succulent forms. Illustrated here is E. splendens which is one of the more woody species. The red petal-like bracts are freely produced over a long period

(Top)
Flower buds produced on a plant of Gymnocaly-cium calochlorum   The protruberance or 'chin' below the areoles is a feature of this genus

(Bottom)
The red 'turbans' are plants of Gymnocalycium optima rubra. As they do not contain chlorophyll and are unable to exist on their own, they are grafted on to a stock from another cactus

(Top)
Grafting of cacti can produce some fascinating combinations (see bottom illustration, page 95). Here, the base of the scion is being pared to remove any ragged edges

(Bottom)
The top has been removed from the plant which is to act as the stock. The scion is held to show the corresponding cut surface

(Top)
The scion is placed on the stock so that the cut surfaces are pressed firmly on to each other. It is important to make sure that the scion is in close contact with the stock

(Bottom)
A piece of weighted twine is used to hold the two parts together. Union should take place in a week or two

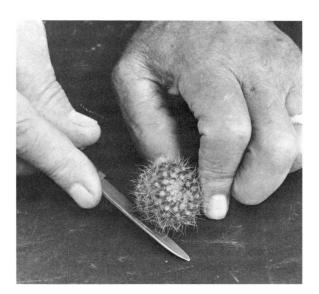

CHAPTER TEN

pests and diseases

PESTS

Succulents are attacked by the same pests as most greenhouse plants, but these are quite easily dealt with provided excessive infestation is not allowed to occur. Routine individual examination and treatment are best, and all-over spraying or fumigation should only be a last resort.

Ants These may disturb and damage roots, and sometimes introduce greenfly. *Control :* The best thing is to find the nest and destroy it with boiling water or by pouring in carbon disulphide, or at least find and block their entry into the greenhouse. Otherwise use a proprietary ant-killer or derris dust.

Aphids The ordinary greenfly may attack succulents: a watch should be kept when there is a garden infestation. *Control :* Spray with dimethoate or malathion.

Mealy bug This is the commonest pest. A relation of the aphid, it is white, woolly and about ⅛ in. long. *Control :* Pick off individual insects with a small paint-brush dipped in soapy water. Spray with an insecticide such as dimethoate or malathion.

Red spider If plants have white or yellow markings, a webbed appearance, or begin to shrivel, red spider should be suspected (but see also Starvation, page 98). These tiny red mites can only be seen under a lens. *Control :* Spray with derris, dimethoate or malathion, or fumigate with azobenzene.

Root mealy bug Similar to mealy bug, but infests roots, making white woolly patches. If the plant looks unhealthy, examine the roots. *Control :* The soil must be shaken off (and destroyed) and the pests removed as much as possible. The roots should then be dipped into dimethoate or malathion solution. As a deterrent, the plants may be watered with a malathion solution, or with a prepared nicotine emulsion, or a few crystals of paradichlorbenzene or flakes of naphthalene may be placed among the crocks.

Scale insects Small waxy mounds about ⅛ in. across are the covering of scale insects, a kind of aphid that settles down in one place. *Control :* Spray with dimethoate or malathion. It is best to use a paint-brush soaked in the insecticidal solution to remove the scale bodily, or to move each scale with a blunt stick, taking care not to damage the plant.

Slugs and snails Considerable damage can be done by these creatures, and regular inspection should be made. *Control :* Proprietary meta-and-bran baits.

Thrips Small grey or white marks on plants may be caused by these insects, which are very thin, about ⅛ in. long, and jump. *Control :* Spray with dimethoate or malathion.

Woodlice These pests may attack plants, especially seedlings. *Control :* Use BHC dust, or attract the pests by placing a scooped-out turnip or potato nearby.

Note : It is important that all insecticides are handled with great care. Follow maker's instructions at all times, especially when fumigating. Do not spray in full sunlight; early in the day is best.

Dimethoate is a systemic insecticide which passes into the sap of the plants. Other materials mentioned are contact poisons and remain on the leaf surfaces. Do not spray crassulas or kalanchoës with malathion.

DISEASES

The diseases of succulents are perhaps more difficult to deal with, because their main cause is faulty cultivation.

Damping-off Seedlings of succulents may suffer from damping-off, when they rot at the base and fall over. Care in watering, adequate ventilation and sterilised compost will help to avert this; as an additional precaution, Cheshunt compound should be used on the seed-pans – say every month.

Dry rot This is a mysterious disease, in which the plants shrivel and parts become dry and withered. Even if such parts are removed, the rest of the plant usually dies. It is commonest in the resting period, and the only thing to do is to try to force the plant into growth, *slowly*, with extra warmth and additional watering.

Frost Frost damage is superficially similar to soft rot, though in bad cases the result is a slimy mass and the plant is finished. Slightly frosted plants should be thawed out slowly, any damaged part removed, and dusted as suggested for soft rot.

Mildew There is a kind of mildew which attacks cacti, producing the usual greyish film on the surface. It occurs in over-damp, airless conditions; the plant can be cleaned up with thiram, dinocap or a colloidal copper spray.

Soft rot Rotting, usually at the base, may be due to various causes. The most common is over-watering, especially if associated with a heavy soil or bad drainage. Rotting at the top of a plant is often due to water lodging there. Rot may also follow soft growth caused by unbalanced feeding, or by fermenting material in the soil such as partly decayed manure. Excessive salt in the soil or an excess of any single chemical may have the same effect. Some plants dislike full sun and may be scorched on a cloudless day; such scorch may become a seat of rot. Scorch may also occasionally follow careless watering, which leaves drops of water on the plants that act as lenses in the sun. Careless removal of cuttings or offsets may result in rot.

All these sorts of decay must be checked by removal of the infected area. In a cactus the flesh is often streaky round the soft area; these streaks must be cut right out. Sometimes the damaged area can be treated by dusting with powdered charcoal or flowers of sulphur; usually the plant is so much mutilated that only a healthy upper part is left. Fortunately most succulents root readily as cuttings, and this is the thing to do with such upper parts (see page 90). If the root is unaffected, it should be dusted and may sprout afresh.

Corky, brown patches and orange or brown spotting, the latter especially on opuntias, indicates a past severe check, such as a chill, or physical damage.

Starvation When a plant has been in a pot too long the soil becomes replaced with roots. Starvation and drying out result, and the plant may begin to wither, go yellow and finally rot. Turn the plant out, remove the dead roots, cut back the top to healthy tissue and repot.

Infrequent repotting and the starvation which results are probably the most usual causes of bad health among succulents.

(Right)
The startling flowers of the Christmas Cactus,
***Schlumbergera buckleyi* ; to achieve this effect**
it must be grown in an equable temperature

list of succulent genera

In the list that follows I have briefly described 72 genera and their cultivation, mainly those which are relatively easy to grow and obtain. Synonyms are not mentioned except where really necessary. The following abbreviations are used:

T. : Temperature   Min. : Minimum
R. : Resting period   Max. : Maximum
P. : Propagation   W.   : Winter

The resting period may vary from species to species, and is only a generalisation; cultivation should never rely on the calendar (see page 86). Where no resting period is indicated or specific details about watering or temperature are not given, the average treatment described in Chapter Eight should be followed. Since with few exceptions all cacti can be readily increased from both seeds and cuttings, and offsets where produced, no specific details of propagation are given for these.

Adromischus *(Crassulaceae)* Low-growing plants, sometimes with short stems, and leaves varying from flat and spoon-shaped to fat and club-shaped or rounded; often nicely mottled, from $\frac{1}{2}$ – 4 in. long. Flowers small, in spikes or clusters, pink or white. All are worth growing. Min. W.T., 7° C. (45° F.). P., seed, stem cuttings or leaves.

Aeonium *(Crassulaceae)* Attractive plants making tight rosettes, similar to the hardy *Sempervivum*, but tender and often with long branching stems. The leaves, sometimes toothed or edged with hairs, are less fleshy, and the rosettes are open, bowl-shaped or, as in *A. tabulaeforme*, quite flat. The small bright flowers, red, pink, white or yellow, are packed into much-branched clusters, often produced only after several years. The rosettes that produce flowers die afterwards. Some (e.g. *A. canariense*, *A. nobile*) make large rosettes up to 2 ft. across, and correspondingly large flower-heads. Others (e.g. *A. domesticum*) make nice little miniature trees.

Easy and worth-while to grow, and thrive in rooms. In winter only frost protection is needed but do not exceed 10° C. (50° F.). P., seed, very quick from cuttings.

Agave *(Agavaceae)* Rosette plants, usually with very hard leaves with spines along the edges, often variegated with white, yellow, pink or pale green. The leaves are commonly broadly lanceolate but occasionally very narrow. A trunk is sometimes formed. Some eventually grow to great size. Flowers on upright spikes, often only appearing after many years; individual rosettes die after flowering. Most make attractive pot plants when small. Easy to grow, many needing only frost protection, and resist neglect; useful in tubs in the summer. P., seed, offsets.

continued on page 104

(Right)
Agave americana marginata aurea, a large-growing rosette plant with yellow-edged leaves

(Top)

A cluster of flowers on *Bryophyllum tubiflorum*. This plant grows 2–3 feet tall and is easily propagated from the plantlets at the ends of the cylindrical leaves

(Bottom)

Easily grown, but requiring plenty of water in summer, *Aeonium domesticum*, with its attractive rosette leaf form, is a good plant for a bowl

(Top)

The Peanut Cactus, *Chamaecereus sylvestrii*, produces myriads of flowers. Easy to grow, this is the ideal plant for the beginner

(Bottom)

All species of *Coryphantha* produce flowers readily on fully grown plants; *C. elephantidens*, an especially beautiful example, is illustrated

(Top)
A good plant for a hanging basket, the trailing stems of *Aporocactus flagelliformis* bear many flowers in May

(Bottom)
One of the aptly named Star Cacti, *Astrophytum asterias* has a flat stone-like body on which the white woolly areoles (spineless in this species) can be seen

(Top)
Delosperma lehmannii is an easily-grown, compact plant which bears pale yellow flowers

(Bottom)
Conophytum nobile is a species of one of the most fascinating succulent genera. All are easy to grow and readily produce flowers

Aloe *(Liliaceae)* Rather dull plants, usually forming rosettes, or sometimes with leaves in two rows, and frequently with long stems. Rosettes similar to agaves, but leaves usually fewer, often toothed. Flowers, sometimes showy, red, orange or yellow, on long stalks. Commonly cultivated is *A. variegata*, the Partridge Breast Aloe, with stubby dark green leaves with many white marks. Tough, easy plants, good in rooms; frost protection only; plenty of water in summer. P., seed, offsets, sometimes from leaf cuttings. Repot every year in late summer.

Aporocactus *(Cactaceae)* The Rat's-tail Cacti, epiphytes with long, trailing, ribbed stems up to 3 ft. or more, around ½ in. thick, covered with small spines. Need growing in a basket or do well grafted on a columnar cactus such as *Nyctocereus serpentinus* or *Selenicereus* spp. The pink or red flowers, about 3 in. long, appear in late spring. Best known is *A. flagelliformis*. Prefer a rich, peaty, lime-free soil, with cow manure and plenty of root space. Wet and warm in the growing season. Min. W.T., 10° C. (50° F.).

Argyroderma *(Aizoaceae)* Small stemless plants, usually making only one or two pairs of thick leaves, each pair joined at the base; often forming clumps. The leaves are generally rounded outside and flat on the inner faces of the pair, but are sometimes fingerlike (e.g. *A. braunsii*). Flower freely, in various colours. Min. W.T., 10° C. (50° F.). R., mainly W., varies with species: all but dry. P., seed.

Astrophytum *(Cactaceae)* The Star Cacti, globular, with four to eight ribs, usually well marked, spineless in *A. asterias* and *A. myriostigma*, with stiff spines in *A. ornatum* and papery spines in *A. capricorne*. The four-ribbed *A. myriostigma quadricostata* is sometimes called Parson's Cap. The bodies are covered with tiny white tufts. The flowers are large and yellow. Water with care. Easily grown and very attractive.

(Below)
An attractive, low-growing plant, *Adromischus festivus* has elongated mottled leaves ending in a thin wavy edge. Sun loving, these plants usually flower freely in late spring and summer

(Below)
One of the best known of the aloes, *A. variegata*, the Partridge Breast Aloe, derives its common name from the strikingly marked green and white leaves. The coral-coloured flowers are produced in spring

(Below)
The Old Man Cactus is a decidedly apt common name for *Cephalocereus senilis*. This plant has considerable curiosity value because of its 'wig' of long white hairs

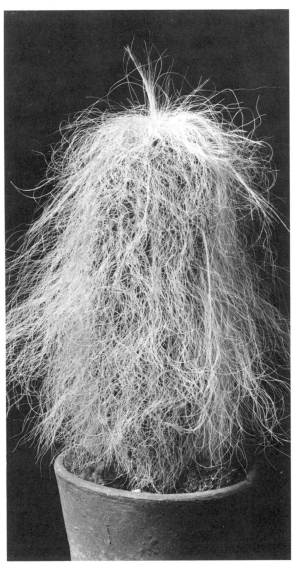

(Top)
Echeveria retusa hybrida is one of the many beautiful plants to be found in this genus. All can be grown in well-lit rooms but they do not like central heating

(Bottom)
The strikingly coloured leaf rosettes of *Echeveria gibbiflora metallica* ensure that it is an attractive as well as a useful plant for growing in a bowl garden

(Right)
A fine grouping of *Echinocactus grusonii*: the large specimen is perhaps a century old

Bryophyllum *(Crassulaceae)* Related to *Kalanchoë* and by some botanists now included in that genus. Tall, bushy plants, often shrubby in nature, making plantlets in the leaf-notches or, in *B. proliferum*, among the flowers, which are quite large, in clusters, appearing usually in autumn or winter. *B. crenatum* has oval leaves and red flowers; *B. daigremontianum*, the Mexican Hat, has long triangular leaves and yellow or pink flowers; *B. tubiflorum* has long, thin, cylindrical leaves with plantlets at the end, and orange flowers. They make nice room plants, needing rich soil and only slight heat in winter. P., seeds or plantlets; the latter root anywhere!

Carpobrotus *(Aizoaceae)* *C. edulis*, the Hottentot Fig, with large white, magenta or yellow flowers and long, thick, triangular leaves, is a plant often naturalised on our south and south-west coasts. Other species are similar. Strong-growing plants, almost hardy, suitable for planting out in frost-free places; not so satisfactory and shy-flowering, in pots. Very rich soil. P., cuttings best.

Cephalocereus *(Cactaceae)* Large columnar cacti, usually woolly or hairy, especially at the top, and with spines. The wool and spines only develop well on old plants. The flowers are small. Though there are scores of species, the only one commonly grown is *C. senilis*, the Old Man. All are rather tricky; water sparingly. Add extra limestone to the compost. Min. W.T., 7° C. (45° F.).

Cereus *(Cactaceae)* Large plants with ribbed or angular spines, columnar stems, often bluish. The flowers are large and open at night. Many of the specimens in commerce are hybrids. The most commonly seen species include steely-blue *C. chalybaeus*, with red and white flowers 7 or 8 in. long; bluish-green *C. jamacaru*; and *C. peruvianus*, which has several cristate forms. Good stock for grafting. All species are easily grown.

(Below)

Cleistocactus strausii has a covering of small shining white spines and makes a handsome plant. It is fairly quick growing and likes warmth and sunshine

Ceropegia *(Asclepiadaceae)* Odd plants, either fleshy, upright and leafless, or twiners, usually with opposite leaves. Roots often tuberous. Flowers 5-lobed, the lobes generally joined to each other at the tips; some are very curious, e.g. *C. haygarthii* and *C. sandersonii*. Hearts Entangled, *C. woodii*, is a creeper making tubers among the small heart-shaped leaves. Easy to grow, even in rooms; climbers best in hanging baskets. Soil rich, with extra humus. Min. W.T., 10° C. (50° F.). P., seeds, cuttings or aerial tubers if formed.

Chamaecereus *(Cactaceae)* The only species, *C. sylvestrii*, is the popular Peanut Cactus. It is small, making a clump of branching, more or less prostrate pale green stems up to 6 in. long and 1 in. thick, with small white spines. In spring the scarlet flowers, about 2½ in. long and 1½ in. across, are profusely produced. There are cristate forms and a yellow-coloured form. Nearly hardy, and best kept between 1 – 4° C. (33 – 40° F.) in winter. Easy for rooms.

Cheiridopsis *(Aizoaceae)* An interesting genus with many very fleshy species of varying shape. One to three pairs of leaves, each pair different. Some species make longish, triangular leaves; others have a boat-shaped pair of basal leaves and short, rounded central pair; others are small and rounded. Quite difficult, needing moderate watering only in the growing period, but worth specialised study. R., early spring to late summer, quite dry. Min. W.T., 10° C. (50° F.). P., seed.

Cissus *(Vitaceae)* Most cissus are shrubby climbers related to the grape, and there are some succulent climbers (e.g. *C. cactiformis*, *C. quadrangularis*) with four-angled, ribbed, jointed stems, with leaves and tendrils at lobes and ends, which are quite easy to grow in a cool house. P., cuttings.

The really succulent species, however, are rare, peculiar and difficult. Examples are *C. bainesii*, *C. hypoleuca*, *C. juttae*. For much of the year, when they should be kept quite dry, they exist as conical or barrel-shaped stems with whitish, peeling skin, from 2 – 12 ft. high in nature but rarely over 1 ft. in cultivation. In winter, when they should be lightly watered, they produce large, toothed, glossy leaves in a tuft, and sometimes a spray of tiny flowers followed by berries. Maximum sun; soil poor, very porous. Min. W.T., 10° C. (50° F.). P., seed.

Cleistocactus *(Cactaceae)* Columnar or sometimes prostrate, many-ribbed, up to 6 ft. tall but only 1 or 2 in. thick. The flowers are narrow and tubular, about 2 in. long. *C. strausii* is a beautiful plant covered with small white bristles, and has red flowers. The species like a rich, peaty soil, and will stand 8° C. (15° F.) of frost if dry at the roots.

Conophytum *(Aizoaceae)* One of the largest and most drought-adapted genera in the family, entirely composed of small plant-bodies, the basic pair of leaves being almost entirely merged. A few form stems when aged, and these make tap-roots. Most make clumps at ground level. The bodies are round, conical, cylindrical or ovate; some have no division; some a tiny slit in the top; others have more or less pronounced lobes. The flowers emerge from the centre of the top and are $\frac{1}{2} - 1\frac{1}{4}$ in. across. They are easy to grow, will flower in rooms and can be increased rapidly. Min. W.T., 10 C. (50°F.). R., September/October–July, when the outer skin becomes very withered; keep almost dry September–December; quite dry January–June/July. P., seed, division.

Coryphantha *(Cactaceae)* A large genus of low cylindrical or globular plants with more or less pronounced tubercles, resembling *Mammillaria*, but separated because of a groove in the upper surface of the tubercles. The flowers are often large, usually yellow. Prefer a peaty compost. Easy to grow.

Cotyledon *(Crassulaceae)* A confused genus close to many other members of the family, containing various types of plant. Most are attractive, easy and good indoors, W.T., min. 6° C. (42° F.), max. 10° C. (50° F.). These include species such as *C. macrantha, orbiculata* and *undulata*, which resemble the shrubby crassulas. Another group, including *C. reticulata* and *wallichii*, resemble miniature palms, with clumps of thin cylindrical leaves at the ends of long stems. These are more fussy, with a min. W.T. of 10° C. (50° F.), and needing to be kept fully dry in the summer rest period. The flowers are carried in clusters. P., seed, quickly from cuttings, less easily from leaves.

Crassula *(Crassulaceae)* A large genus of attractive plants of various forms, most worth cultivation. Leaves almost always opposite, often in cruciform arrangement, but may be spread out on long stems or tightly packed together. The small flowers in clusters are pink, white, rarely yellow. Typical of the shrubby species are *C. arborescens, argentea* and *lactea*, stout plants with fleshy, roughly spoon-shaped leaves. In *C. perforata* the greyish, lanceolate leaves are closely packed in alternate pairs. *C. falcata* has rhomboidal, crosswise-upright leaves, the whole plant being flattened in one vertical plane. It has large clusters of carmine flowers.

Some are trailers, attractive in baskets, such as *C. rupestris, corallina* and *spathulata* in which small leaves, joined together at the base, are strung like beads on long stems.

In *C. lycopodioides* the tiny leaves are packed into erect, square stems up to 2 ft. high and $\frac{1}{4}$ in. thick. This is similar in structure to the 'mimicry' forms, such as *C. pyramidalis, C. columnaris, C. quadrangularis, C. arta, C. teres*; in these the stem is square or rounded, and the leaves are so close that a nearly smooth surface results. Lastly there is a group of low-growing, very succulent forms, including *C. cornuta, C. tabularis*, and *C. tecta*.

continued on page 112

109

(Left)
The spectacular flowers of *Epiphyllum* London Delight are typical of those produced by the hybrid group of Orchid Cacti

(Right)
The boat-shaped, toothed leaves have earned for this plant the name Tiger's Jaw. Botanically it is *Faucaria tigrina*

(Below)
Fenestraria rhopalophylla, an interesting succulent belonging to the group of 'window' plants. This is the less common of the two species usually grown

(Top)

The bizarre palm-like appearance of *Cotyledon wallichii* is attributable to the clusters of cylindrical leaves at the ends of the considerably thickened stems

(Bottom)

A member of a very variable genus, *Crassula argentea* has glossy dark green leaves and pale pink flowers. It eventually forms an attractive large bush

Most of the species are easy to grow and do well in rooms, with a max. W.T. of 10° C. (50° F.). The 'mimicry' forms are for the expert, and should be kept to the greenhouse, needing a min. W.T. of 10° C. (50° F.), and to be rested, nearly dry, in our summer. The last-mentioned, fleshy forms need similar conditions and rest in our winter. P., seed, readily by cuttings, also from leaves.

Delosperma *(Aizoaceae)* Most are small shrubs with smallish leaves, often covered with raised dots and hairs, giving a silvery, sparkling look. Commonest is *D. echinatum*. They flower freely and for many months, with small whitish or reddish blooms. W.T. min. 6° C. (42° F.), max. 10° C. (50° F.). P., seeds, cuttings.

Dorotheanthus *(Aizoaceae)* The Livingstone Daisy, a delightful and showy little annual. Seedsmen sell it as *Mesembryanthemum criniflorum*, but the packet usually contains hybrids which produce flowers white, buff, pink or carmine, sometimes banded in two colours, about $1\frac{1}{2}$ in. across. These are superior to the species *D. criniflorus* and *D. gramineus*, and varieties of the latter. They are classed as half-hardy annuals, but are quite tough and may be sown in cold frames in March or where they are to grow in mid-April or later. Thin out well. A well-drained sandy soil is best and a sunny position essential for the flowers to open properly. Pick off dead flowers for continuous display.

Drosanthemum *(Aizoaceae)* Gay shrubby plants with small cylindrical to triangular leaves covered with sparkling raised dots. The rather small red or white flowers are very freely produced, and the plants are useful for bedding out. W.T. min. 6° C. (42° F.), max. 10° C. (50° F.). P., seed, cuttings.

Echeveria *(Crassulaceae)* A large genus (with many synonyms) of attractive rosette plants, sometimes on stems, which make large clumps quite quickly. Leaves often waxy or glaucous. The dainty urn-shaped flowers, red, orange, yellow or white, are carried on long stems. Most flower in summer, but some in winter. *E. glauca* is often used for carpet-bedding. All are attractive; recommended are *E. gibbiflora, perelegans, gigantea* (nearly 2 ft. across), *setosa, retusa* and *puberula*. Best kept under glass are *E. cotyledon, densiflora* and *farinosa*. They will grow in rooms, but the flowers may then dry up before opening. W.T. min. 6° C. (42° F.), max. 10° C. (50° F.); cold frames will do for bedders, kept almost dry. P., seed, cuttings of almost any part.

Echinocactus *(Cactaceae)* Round or barrel-shaped, flattened at the top, covered with fearsome spines. The flowers are smallish, seldom produced in pots, although *E. horizonthalonius* will do so when quite young. *E. grusonii* is common; it will grow to nearly 3 ft. across and has interlacing golden spikes up to 3 in. long. Rich soil preferred.

Echinocereus *(Cactaceae)* A large genus with soft fleshy stems up to 15 in. long and 1 – 3 in. thick, erect or prostrate, making spreading clumps. Some have spines, others none. The flowers, white, yellow, red or purple, are fairly large. They are easy to grow and many are quite hardy. There is little to choose between the many attractive species. W.T., 1 – 4° C. (33 – 40° F.). Cuttings should be taken in late June and July.

Echinopsis *(Cactaceae)* A popular window-sill plant. Usually round or cylindrical, rarely columnar; spiny, with marked ribs. Characteristically flower very freely even when young, with large, long-tubed pink or white flowers of great beauty. Many hybrids exist. Occasional sports occur which produce myriads of offsets; these plants seldom flower. Easy to grow; many fairly hardy.

Epiphyllum *(Cactaceae)* Shrubby epiphytes with flat or 3-angled leaf-like joints, often notched, seldom spiny. In the species the flowers are usually small and open at night;

(Top)
One of the many plant forms to be found among the euphorbias, *E. horrida* bears a striking resemblance to a cactus. The thorns are formed from old inflorescences

(Bottom)
Another euphorbia, this time *E. obesa*. A cluster of flowers can be seen at the top of the round stem, which is grey-green with reddish stripes

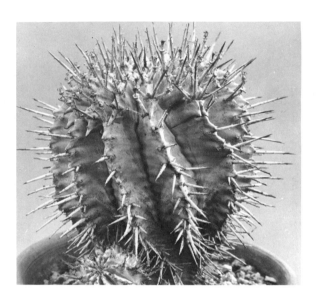

it is the hybrids, often crosses with *Helio-cereus* or the *Hylocereus* tribe, and commonly called Orchid Cacti, which are best known, with large very beautiful flowers of almost every colour except blue. Sometimes grafted on *Hylocereus undatus*. They like rich but porous soil (see page 84), half-shade, plenty of water when growing, fairly dry when not. Watering should be reduced for a few weeks after flowering. They appreciate a lot of air in summer and, unlike most succulents, a damp atmosphere obtained by regular syringing. Hence they are more suitable for growing in a mixed greenhouse than with other succulents. Min. W.T., 7° C. (45° F.).

Euphorbia *(Euphorbiaceae)* This is one of the largest genera of plants and includes a number of diverse succulent forms. Many make tree-like growth, and many resemble cacti, apart from the flowers, which are usually insignificant. It is difficult to make a selection from at least 100 succulent species. Some are more woody than succulent, like the brilliant red-flowered *E. splendens* and *E. bojeri*, often called Crown of Thorns. Other woody species with leaves are *E. alcicornis, canariensis, lophogona* – the latter with white leaves and red stalks.

Among the cactiform are the jointed, 4-angled *E. abyssinica* and *E. similis*; 3-winged, fierce-spined *E. grandicornis*; and square-stemmed *E. resinifera*. *E. horrida* is like a spherical cactus. *E. caput-medusae* has radiating branches from a central head. There is a tuberous-rooted group, including *E. aequoris*, almost totally buried, and *E. namibensis* with parsnip-like root and many short, bristly branches. Of most interest, perhaps, are the very fleshy forms, such as the spherical or oval *E. obesa*. The prominently ribbed *E. meloformis* resembles an astrophytum. *E. bupleurifolia* is an example of a type which is covered with scales, which are in fact leaf-cushions, and has long narrow leaves on top.

(Left)
The leaves of *Gasteria verrucosa* are covered with raised white dots

(Centre left)
Gymnocalycium baldianum is one of a genus of plants that are all easy to cultivate

(Bottom left)
The interlaced, heavy armament of spines of *Ferocactus acanthodes* is typical of this group of cacti, all of which are worth growing

(Below)
The curious rose bud-shaped rosette of *Greenovia aurea*, shown here during the resting season

In fact, the euphorbias should be in any collection, and are a perfect subject for a specialised one. They are mainly easy to grow, needing a min. W.T. of 7° C. (45° F.), and do well in rooms. The leafy forms are rich feeders and like much water in summer; the really succulent ones need special care with drainage and watering – usually no water in winter. P., seed, cuttings. Caution – the typical milky juice (latex) is poisonous and must be kept from eye, mouth or any cut.

Faucaria *(Aizoaceae)* Small clump-forming plants with 1 – 3 pairs of thick, triangular leaves, which have teeth or spines on the edges – hence the apt name Tiger's Jaw. The large yellow flowers appear in autumn. Easy to grow, good in rooms. W.T. min. 10° C. (50° F.), max. 13° C. (55° F.). R., spring and summer. Free watering in winter, sparingly in summer. P., best from seed, also cuttings.

Fenestraria *(Aizoaceae)* Difficult but interesting; a 'window-plant' (see page 68), forming large clumps of leaves, about 1 in. long, round in section and thickening towards the flattish translucent top. In nature these are buried up to the top. The pale orange flowers are very large – up to 3 in. across – in the commonest species, *F. aurantiaca*. Need bright position; compost mainly of sand. Min. W.T., 6° C. (42° F.). R., September/October–February, when very little watering is required. Little water even in growing period. P., seed, or division of clumps, but resents disturbance, including repotting.

Ferocactus *(Cactaceae)* Spherical to cylindrical plants, some becoming very large (e.g. *F. diguettii*, 12 ft. high, 3 ft. across), with marked ribs, and a heavy array of long thick spines, usually attractively coloured, the central one often hooked and sometimes 5 in. long. The flowers are relatively small but showy, red, yellow or violet. All are worth growing. They like heavy, rubbly compost, and should be watered very cautiously.

(Top)
The rosette-shaped *Haworthia cooperi* is remarkable for its light green leaves, which are translucent at the tips

(Bottom)
The felted leaves of *Kalanchoë tomentosa* are silvery white with scorched-looking brown markings around the leaf edges

Gasteria *(Liliaceae)* Typically with thick, tongue-like, pointed leaves in two ascending rows, sometimes spirally twisted when older; a few make rosettes. The leaves are often covered with white tubercles (e.g. *G. verrucosa*). The quite showy flowers are like those of *Aloe*, and cultivation is the same, though they dislike direct sunlight. *G. neliae* is attractive, with horny edge and regular white flecks on bright green leaves. *G. acinacifolia* forms a rosette of white-spotted, foot-long leaves. Tough plants, useful in rooms. P., seed, offsets, leaf cuttings.

Gibbaeum *(Aizoaceae)* Interesting but difficult; very succulent plants with 1 or 2 pairs of leaves, making clumps. Some are roughly spherical (e.g. *G. album*, *G. pilosulum*); some egg-shaped (e.g. *G. dispar*); some have finger-shaped leaves, short and blunt in *G. perviride*, longer in *G. pubescens* and more angular in *G. nelii*. *G. velutinum* makes flat, triangular leaves. Most are curious in that the leaves of a pair are of different sizes, and the division between them is oblique. Small white or pink flowers. Growing period varies between species, from winter to early summer; water lightly then, keep quite dry when resting. Min. W.T., 10° C. (50° F.). P., seed, cuttings.

Glottiphyllum *(Aizoaceae)* The name means 'tongue-leaf' and is apt. The leaves are usually longer than wide, but sometimes short and broad, thick, fleshy, irregular, very soft and waxy to touch, generally a bright green; they typically radiate at ground level from a number of stem-like growths, and flower freely with large yellow blooms. Little to choose between species except leaf-shape. Easy to grow. R., February–May, quite dry and cool. Moderate water in growing period. P., seed (may not be true); cuttings best.

Greenovia *(Crassulaceae)* Very similar to *Aeonium*, but always on short stems; cultivation the same. Rosettes which have flowered die. Few species: *G. aizoon* has white-haired rosettes $2\frac{1}{2}$ in. across. *G. aurea* makes cushions of large glaucous rosettes and *G. gracilis* has small rosettes, in each case like rosebuds. Good room plants. W.T. min. 6° C. (42° F.), max. 10° C. (50° F.). R., late summer–winter, when rosettes close up; keep fairly dry. P., seed, quicker from cuttings.

Gymnocalycium *(Cactaceae)* Curious but attractive globular cacti, ranging from 1 – 12 in. across, but mainly small, with rounded ribs divided into low tubercles, each carrying a few smallish spines. Many species and hybrids, all decorative, with quite large white or pink flowers (red in *G. baldianum*), usually freely produced and on young plants. Easy to grow; rich soil, much water in the summer. Many are fairly hardy; they prefer half-shade.

Haworthia *(Liliaceae)* Mainly rosette plants, some remaining low, some ascending, a few with leaves in two rows. Some have very hard, tubercled leaves, as *H. margaritifera* and *H. fasciata*; some are bristly (*H. altilinea*); others have soft, translucent, triangular leaves, such as *H. cooperi* and *cymbiformis*, and the netted *H. tessellata*. In various fleshy forms the rosettes are, in nature, buried to expose only the flat leaf-ends, as with *H. retusa* and the most adapted forms, *H. maughanii* – a little like *Fenestraria* – and *H. truncata*, with two rows of thick, flattened, crowded leaves. The long-stalked flowers are insignificant. Most are easy to grow and thrive in rooms, but the last two mentioned need treatment more as for *Lithops*. Otherwise cultivation as for *Aloe*. W.T. min. 6° C. (42° F.), max. 13° C. (55° F.). R., winter, when water moderately. P., seed, offsets. Repot in late summer.

Heliocereus *(Cactaceae)* Usually trailers, with thin stems, remarkable for their large, beautiful, strong-scented flowers, for which they are called the Sun Cacti. These may be red, often with touches of green, purple or white, and up to 6 in. long. *H. speciosus* is usually seen, and is one of the parents of many

(Top)
Kleinia articulata, the Candle Plant, is the most popular of the kleinias. The glaucous, jointed stems break and root readily, and for a short season carry ivy-like leaves

(Bottom)
Most of the notocactus are free flowering and very hardy. The large yellow and red flowers of *N. floricomus* provide a spectacular display

of the hybrid epiphyllums. Like them, these plants need heat, some air moisture, peaty soil and half-shade. A little bonemeal may be given. Min. W.T., 7° C. (45° F.).

Hylocereus *(Cactaceae)* Epiphytic plants with aerial roots; stems long-jointed, notched, angular or winged, with a few small spines. The usually nocturnal flowers, often scented, have white petals and red, purple or green sepals, are sometimes very freely produced, and are large – generally 6–8 in. and in some cases 12 in. long. The fruits are also large. They need warmth, air moisture and a free root-run to flower, and prefer very rich, peaty soil, without lime, and half-shade. *H. undatus* and *H. triangularis* are commonly seen, and are often used as grafting stocks for pendulous plants.

Kalanchoë *(Crassulaceae)* Closely related to *Bryophyllum*, but not producing adventitious buds. Erect, sub-shrubby plants, often becoming large, with opposite leaves and large clusters of small bright flowers, white, red or yellow. The flower-bearing shoots die afterwards, but new growths arise at the base. *K. blossfeldiana*, with scarlet flowers in winter and spring, is grown commercially, and *K. flammea* (orange-red) and *K. pumila* (pink) are equally good value. Modern hybrids have larger flowers. In others the leaves are the main attraction: *K. grandiflora* has bluish, rounded, notched leaves; *K. marmorata* greyish leaves of similar shape with handsome brown markings; *K. pruinosa* long, pointed, notched, glaucous leaves; *K. tomentosa* is covered with silvery fur, reddish-brown at the leaf-tips; while *K. beharensis* soon grows large with big, felted, wavy leaves.

Easy to grow, usually good in rooms. The flowering kinds are grown rather like *Rochea coccinea*, being kept in shaded frames and cut back in late June. W.T. min. 6° C. (42° F.), max. 10° C. (50° F.). P., seed, cuttings.

Kleinia *(Compositae)* A genus of several very

interesting plants, most quite easy to grow in rooms. Modern classification places these under *Senecio*. The most commonly seen is *K. articulata*, the Candle Plant, which has blue-grey, jointed stems and, for a short season, ivy-shaped leaves. *K. anteuphorbium* has very long joints and lanceolate, silver-grey leaves. *K. ficoides* and *K. repens* are more prostrate plants, with narrow leaves and rigid joints. *K. neriifolia*, which eventually makes a 10-ft. bush, looks like a miniature palm-tree. Most interesting is *K. gomphophylla*, which has prostrate stems rooting as they go, with leaves like green acorns. They have pale stripes which are in fact 'sun-windows'. This is a desert plant and needs less water than the others, but all need cautious watering, particularly *K. tomentosa*, a very attractive plant forming 12-in. clumps with cylindrical leaves, pointed at both ends, about 1½ in. long, the whole covered with close white felt. It is very sensitive to changes of temperature. Keep all kleinias nearly dry in summer.

W.T., min. 6° C. (42° F.), max. 10° C. (50° F.). P., seed or cuttings; the joints, which are easily detached, root rapidly. Repot in early autumn.

Lampranthus *(Aizoaceae)* More or less shrubby plants, with fairly distant leaves, usually long and narrow. They flower freely during most of the summer, and are much used for bedding, particularly in milder localities. They are also attractive pot and basket plants. The nurseryman will call most of them *Mesembryanthemum*. There are very many attractive species, most with 2- or 3-in. flowers. Among the pink ones are *L. blandus*, *roseus* and *falciformis*; reds include scarlet *L. coccineus*, purple-carmine *L. conspicuus*, purple-red *L. haworthii* and *L. spectabilis*. *L. zeyheri* is a brilliant violet-purple; *L. amoenus* is mauve; *L. glaucus* a large yellow; *L. aurantiacus* is orange; *L. tenuifolius* orange-scarlet; *L. aureus* yellow or orange. All need

(Below)
This young specimen of *Lemaireocereus pruinosus* shows the glaucous colouring which makes these plants particularly attractive

only protection from frost and to be kept nearly dry in winter. They can be overwintered in a light, airy room. P., seed, cuttings best.

Lemaireocereus *(Cactaceae)* Growing into tree-like clumps, with stems 3 – 6 in. thick, and with short, often coloured spines. Most branch freely, but *L. marginatus*, often used as a hedge-plant in Mexico, grows straight up. The ridges of its ribs are topped with wool. Flowers usually small; the species are prized more for their form and colouring, especially good in seedlings. Cultivation as for *Cereus*. Min. W.T., 6°C. (42°F.).

Leuchtenbergia *(Cactaceae)* *L. principis*, the only species, is a remarkable cactus with long root, woody stem and very long triangular tubercles, 5 in. long and $\frac{3}{8}$ in. across, with papery spines 4 in. long at the ends. The yellow flower is $2\frac{1}{2}$ in. across. Easy to grow in porous soil: much water while in growth. Seedlings grow fast, flowering in 4 or 5 years. P., cuttings of tubercles.

Lithops *(Aizoaceae)* A large genus of very fleshy plant-bodies, often coloured and patterned and resembling stones, and in nature buried up to the top, living in the hottest desert conditions. The bodies are conical or cylindrical, and the two leaves which compose each are completely joined, apart from a more or less pronounced cleft in the top. The yellow or white flowers appear in the cleft, and are usually bigger than the body; the top is flat or slightly convex.

The species are all basically similar, but vary in markings and size, the latter from about $\frac{3}{8}$ – $1\frac{3}{4}$ in. in height. In cultivation they often exceed the natural size. It is best to grow them in separate pots and, since they like very hot sun, to sink the pots in a gravelly bed. This avoids root-scorch. Very sandy soil is necessary. Watering should always be cautious, and none given in winter. They can be grown on a sunny window-sill. Min. W.T., 10°C. (50°F.). R., November/January–April/

May. P., seeds; cuttings can also be used or clumps divided.

Lobivia *(Cactaceae)* A large genus of small, round or cylindrical, ribbed, spiny plants, with relatively large flowers, usually red, (*L.nealeana, L.famatimensis, L.hertrichiana*), sometimes orange (*L.drijveriana*), or yellow (*L.haageana* and *L.famatimensis aurantiaca*). There are numerous hybrids. They are very free flowering and easy to grow, preferring some shade and rich, limy soil; cool in winter.

Lophocereus *(Cactaceae)* The one species, *L. schottii*, grows to 15 ft., about $2\frac{1}{2}$ in. thick, with thick spines and many bristles. The flowers are small. It is the monstrous form, often labelled *Cereus* or *Lemaireocereus mieckleyanus*, that is usually grown – an extraordinary sight with irregular ribs, quite spineless and smooth. Water cautiously.

Lophophora *(Cactaceae)* *L. williamsii* is notorious as *mescal* or *peyotl*, the dried form in which it was eaten by the Mexican Indians, since it contains powerful intoxicating and narcotic alkaloids. Fairly easy to grow, it is one of a group (mainly difficult) of cacti which look more like round, grey, scaly potatoes, with low tubercles and wool-bearing areoles. There is a large tap-root. Flowers smallish, pink to white. Needs heavy, porous soil. Rather slow from seed.

Mammillaria *(Cactaceae)* At least 240 species, mainly globular, sometimes cylindrical, all with tubercles, which have spines at the apex and often wool in the axils. Flowers smallish but attractive, usually in a ring round the top, followed by red fruits. There are too many – mostly attractive and easy to grow – to give any list of species. Good room plants. The genus is divided into two sections, one with watery sap and the other with milky sap (which may only be in the body and not the tubercles). The former need plenty of water in summer, the latter less. Many are very winter-hardy if dry.

Mesembryanthemum *(Aizoaceae)* As now understood, this – the original name-genus of the family – is confined entirely to annuals and biennials, of which *Dorotheanthus* (see page 112) and *Mesembryanthemum crystallinum* are often grown. The latter, sometimes called *Cryophytum* or Ice Plant, is grown for its sparkling, spoon-shaped leaves. Nurserymen, however, continue to use the name for many shrubby species, especially *Lampranthus* (see page 119), and it is used loosely to denote any member of the tribe.

Notocactus *(Cactaceae)* Usually globular with flattened top, ribbed, spiny, up to 6 in. across; rarely cylindrical, as is *N. leninghausii*, 3 ft. tall, which is laced with golden bristles. Flowers prolific, up to 3 in. wide, but mostly smaller, mainly yellow. Good species include *N. concinnus, floricomus, ottonis, scopa*. Fairly rich soil. Very hardy.

Ophthalmophyllum *(Aizoaceae)* Small plants, up to $1\frac{1}{2}$ in. high, very like *Lithops*, but with pronounced rounded lobes, often translucent. Flowers pink, reddish or white. Soil should be very sandy. Min. W.T., 10° C. (50 ° F.). R., March–August, quite dry, even for seedlings. P., seed.

Opuntia *(Cactaceae)* About 300 species, divided into four well-marked groups: *Platyopuntia*, the largest, with flattened round or oval joints; *Brasiliopuntia*, with a cylindrical main stem; *Tephrocactus*, with spherical or ovoid joints; and *Cylindropuntia* with columnar stems or long cylindrical joints. Some have primitive, usually awl-shaped leaves which generally fall off soon (e.g. *O. subulata*). Most are spiny, the spines sometimes papery (*O. papyracantha*), but mainly stiff – 4 in. long in *O. aoracantha*. Always with glochids (tiny barbed bristles) in the areoles, which make the plants very unpleasant to handle. Flowers usually large, of various shades of red, orange or yellow, and the fruits mainly large, egg- or pear-shaped, with areoles and spines, often sweet and edible – hence the name Prickly Pears. Few, however, flower freely in pots; *O. compressa* is an honourable exception. Mainly easy to grow in any limy, porous soil, very hardy if winter wet is kept off. A few are difficult. Many are too big for the small collection, but the small kinds are attractive. P., easy from joints.

Oscularia *(Aizoaceae)* Attractive shrubby plants with small greyish leaves, in *O. caulescens* with small teeth and in *O. deltoides* large ones. The small, prolific flowers are pink. Cultivation as for *Lampranthus*.

Pachyphytum *(Crassulaceae)* Attractive plants with thick stems and leaves, usually rounded, ovate or spoon-shaped, purplish, greyish or with a white bloom. Like *Echeveria*, with similar flowers; cultivation the same, but unsuitable for bedding out.

Parodia *(Cactaceae)* Small globular or cylindrical plants, usually 2 or 3 in. through, with marked ribs and small tubercles, very spiny, often woolly. Many flower very freely, with small red or yellow flowers; some are decorative with coloured spines and wool. Attractive plants and very hardy. Cultivation as for *Notocactus*.

Pelargonium *(Geraniaceae)* Our familiar 'geraniums' are of course quite fleshy, and there are several desert forms. The leaves are similar to those of the bedding varieties, and drop in the rest period, which is usually summer. *P. gibbosum* has slender stems and swollen nodes; *P. tetragonum* has angular, jointed stems. *P. echinatum* is quite cactus-like with thorn-like growths. Others with short, much swollen stems are *P. carnosum, crithmifolium* and *paradoxum*. The attractive flowers are white or pink. W.T., 13° C. (55° F.). P., seed, cuttings.

Pereskia *(Cactaceae)* The most primitive cacti, barely succulent, very spiny, with woody stems, and large, glossy leaves which may drop off in the rest period. Areoles large

and woolly. The flowers are 1 – 3 in. across, usually in stalked clusters, white, yellow or pink, often scented, with leaf-like bracts. Fruit pear-shaped, sometimes edible. *P. aculeata godseffiana* is most generally grown, with white flowers and variegated leaves, purple on top, crimson below. Often used as grafting stock for epiphytic cacti. Though rarely grown, they are attractive as well as curious. Need plenty of water and rich heavy loamy soil. Cuttings should be inserted without any drying off.

Pleiospilos *(Aizoaceae)* Plants with 1 – 4 pairs of leaves, making clumps, the leaves usually roughly triangular and very thick, grey to brownish, with small dots, resembling pieces of granite. Flowers large, red or yellow, sometimes several together. *P. bolusii* is often seen, with very broad, short leaves. *P. nelii* has neat hemispherical leaves and *P. magni-punctatus* has green, heavily-keeled leaves. All species are interesting. Prefer very sandy soil. Repot with caution. Min. W.T., 10° C. (50° F.). R., January–September, quite dry. Water freely as leaves develop, then moderately. P., seed, division of clumps.

Portulaca *(Portulacaceae)* *P. grandiflora* is familiar as a half-hardy annual; it has radiating, prostrate stems with cylindrical leaves and bright flowers, which are red in the species, but in the garden hybrids are both single and double and of many colours. Cultivation as for *Dorotheanthus*, but is a little less hardy. Makes an attractive pot plant.

Rebutia *(Cactaceae)* Small, spiny plants, tubercled like *Mammillaria*, 1 or 2 in. across, popular for the freedom with which the small flowers, in a great range of colours, are produced, over a long period. *R. minuscula* is one of the smallest cacti, $1\frac{1}{2}$ in. across, 1 in. high with $1\frac{1}{2}$ in. flowers all spring and summer Very easy to grow.

Rhipsalidopsis *(Cactaceae)* Modern authors may submerge this genus in *Rhipsalis*. The

Easter Cactus, *R. gaertneri*, is a pendulous epiphytic cactus with bright scarlet flowers in spring. (It used to be called *Schlumbergera gaertneri*.) *R. rosea* is a small plant with more open pink flowers, also flowering in spring. Cultivation as for *Epiphyllum*.

Rhipsalis *(Cactaceae)* Epiphytic plants from tropical forests, with cylindrical, flat or angular joints, and woolly bristly areoles. Growths often branching, prostrate or trailing with aerial roots. Small starry flowers, white, pink, red or greenish, with few petals profusely produced in winter. Need overhead spraying and warm humid air conditions, little watering, rich, very peaty but porous soil, and much shade. Suitable for an orchid house, and will grow in orchid compost.

The *Rhipsalis* are noteworthy as the only cactus genus native to Africa and Ceylon as well as America.

Rochea *(Crassulaceae)* *R. coccinea* is the florist's 'Crassula', with stems up to 2 ft. high, thin triangular leaves arranged crosswise and fairly closely packed, and showy tubular carmine flowers in terminal clusters. These appear in early spring if forced, later if not. There are other equally attractive species, in which the flowers may be white, pink, yellow or red. Easy plants, good in rooms. Min. W.T., $4 - 7°$ C. ($40 - 45°$ F.). P., seed, usually from cuttings (best in late spring).

Schlumbergera *(Cactaceae)* The correct name of the Christmas Cactus, so long called *Zygocactus truncatus*, is now accepted to be *Schlumbergera buckleyi*; it is in fact a hybrid of more vigour than its parents. The schlumbergeras are epiphytic, pendulous plants, much branched, with short, flat, notched, leaf-like joints. *S. buckleyi* has deep pink flowers, and there are numerous other hybrids and varieties in white, red, violet, although these are not at present easily available in the trade. The leaf-like stem sections have scalloped edges. In *S. truncata* and its forms,

(Top)
Mammillaria bocasana, one of the many beautiful members of this genus of extremely varied and easily grown plants

(Bottom)
The ophthalmophyllums are small plants, similar to lithops. Shown here is *O. dinteri*, an interesting plant with a translucent tip to the top of each rounded lobe

(Top)
Easily recognised as an opuntia by its typical shape, *O. microdasys pallida* exhibits another feature of this genus—the presence of many tiny barbed bristles (glochids) in the areoles

(Bottom)
The thick-stemmed *Pelargonium crithmifolium* is a truly succulent member of the geranium family and a relative of the popular bedding plants

such as Koenigers Weihnachtsfreude, the flowers are distinctly more zygomorphic — that is, they are largely symmetrical only in the vertical plane, while the leaves have triangular or pointed teeth. The flowers of schlumbergeras, 3 in. long and 1 in. across, are profusely produced in autumn and winter, and last well. Cultivation is as for *Epiphyllum*; plants are good in rooms in equable conditions. They are sometimes grafted on to columnar stock to make a 'standard', or may be grown in hanging baskets.

Sedum *(Crassulaceae)* A genus of at least 500 species, mainly hardy, many commonly grown and a number native to Britain. Some of these can be grown in pots, but tend to grow too large. The tender kinds only are normally included in a greenhouse selection, and these are mainly Mexican, with a few from Madeira. They are all attractive plants, forming loose rosettes or spiral groups of leaves at the end of fleshy stems, and vary from several feet high to small prostrate plants. The leaves are of many shapes and may be green, red, bluish or whitish, and the flowers, usually small in clusters, are of several colours.

Among tall-growing species, which tend to grow straggly, are *S. adolphii, dendroideum, nussbaumeri* and *treleasei*, with large roughly boat-shaped leaves; *S. praealtum*, with long flat leaves; *S. palmeri*, with flat, rounded leaves; and *S. compressum*, with leaves oblanceolate and flattish. Perhaps the most attractive are *S. allantoides, pachyphyllum* and *guatamalense*, the first two whitish, the latter purplish; *S. bellum*, with mealy-white, spoon-shaped leaves; and *S. farinosum*, with mealy, awl-shaped leaves. *S. stahlii* is a small spreading plant with reddish, oval leaves $\frac{1}{2}$ in. long. An unusual species, *S. morganianum*, has pendulous chains of leaves.

All are very easy to grow. W.T., min. 4° C. (40° F.), max. 10° C. (50° F.). P., cuttings, division, usually easy from leaves.

Selenicereus *(Cactaceae)* Trailers or climbers with long, thin, ribbed, branching stems, usually with small spines and aerial roots. The flowers are immense, cup-shaped, around 8 in. long and across, on a long tube. They are white or tinged with red, purple, yellow or green, with radiating sepals and many stamens. Mainly night-flowering, fading soon after daybreak; often very sweetly scented. Old plants will flower over 2 or 3 months. They like a rich, peaty, limy soil, and need some warmth, much water and overhead sprays through spring and summer. *S. grandiflorus* – of which Prof. Borg wrote 'No collection of cacti should be without this marvel of the vegetable kingdom' – is called Queen of the Night; all are known as Moon Cacti.

Sempervivum *(Crassulaceae)* Rosette plants with flower spikes bearing terminal clusters of flowers in many colours, not usually admitted as 'succulents' by the purist owing to their complete hardiness; but they make attractive pot plants for cool conditions. Many have nice red or purplish tints on the leaves and some are 'spider-webbed' (*S. arachnoideum*, etc.). Many plants are hybrids. Porous soil; dry in winter. P., offsets.

Senecio *(Compositae)* The succulent members of this vast genus, which contains the familiar groundsel, now technically includes species treated here under *Kleinia*. Cultivation is identical and most are well worth growing. The adaptations to dry conditions vary a lot. At one extreme is *S. stapeliiformis*, with grey-green stems like a *Stapelia*, but with the typical reddish-orange flower of a weedy Composite – a species needing to be kept very dry. *S. fulgens* has a flask-shaped stem and a spiral bunch of round, flat, glaucous leaves, up to 4 in. long. Several form clumps of short stems and have prostrate branches, like *S. adenocalyx*; *S. scaposus* and *S. vestita* have a rosette of glaucous leaves.

continued on page 128

(Top)
The mealy white leaves of *Sedum bellum* are carried in whorls below the white terminally produced flowers. All of the sedums prefer to be overwintered in a cool temperature

(Bottom)
The small white webbed rosettes of *Sempervivum arachnoideum* make a delightful display when grouped together in a bowl

(Left)
The bizarre flowers of *Stapelia variegata* —here magnified four times—combine with an unpleasant odour to attract pollinating flies

(Top)
Pachyphytum oviferum is a small plant suitable for growing in bowl gardens. The leaves are covered in a thick 'bloom' which gives them the appearance of sugared almonds

(Bottom)
The rebutias, represented here by *R. petersonii*, are one of the easiest group of cacti to cultivate and flower

(Top)
The lovely pendulous flowers of the Easter Cactus, *Rhipsalidopsis gaertneri*. Like *Schlumbergera*, this plant grows best in an even temperature

(Bottom)
All species of *Parodia* are small and very spiny, well illustrated by *P. aureispina*. They are good plants for growing in a container

Stapelia *(Asclepiadaceae)* Many species and hybrids of low branching plants with fleshy, upright, quadrangular stems, toothed on the angles, with short-lived or no leaves. Remarkable for the bizarre, surrealist flowers, usually with a yellowish background more or less marked with brown, dark red or purple, often hairy and usually with a powerful carrion smell that attracts the blowflies that fertilise them – hence the name Carrion Flower. A few are odourless and one or two pleasantly scented. The flowers appear in mid-summer, and have a tube and a bell- or star-shaped corolla, more or less cut into 5 lobes, with a central fleshy ring (the corona); they vary from 1 – 11 in. across. The fruits are horn-shaped, two to a flower, appearing months later. The medium-sized *S. variegata* is most often seen. Easy to grow, even indoors, preferring air moisture in summer and enjoying spraying on hot days. Rich, humus-containing, porous soil. Reduce watering towards autumn, keep fairly dry in winter. Min. W.T., 10° C. (50° F.). P., seed, but this may not be true, best by cuttings.

Stomatium *(Aizoaceae)* Small almost stemless plants with 2 or more pairs of leaves, semi-circular or triangular in section, often with toothed upper edges. Flowers fairly small, yellow. Easy plants. Min. W.T., 7° C. (45° F.). R., autumn-spring. P., seed, cuttings.

Zygocactus See *Schlumbergera*.

---

acknowledgements

This book is based on the completely revised text of the author's highly successful *Amateur Gardening Handbooks: House Plants* and *Cacti and Succulents,* now no longer available.

The Editor is grateful to Mr H.A. Auger of Auger Epiphyllums, Mrs H. Hodgson, Mrs B. Maddams and the House of Rochford for allowing us to photograph their plant collections, and to Mr R. Gilbert, Miss M. Kitchin and Mr and Mrs D. Romer for giving us facilities to photograph plants in their homes.

We would also like to thank the following for providing us with photographs: Bernard Alfieri, *Amateur Gardening*, Arthur Boarder, D.V. Brewerton, P.R. Chapman, Ernest Crowson, Valerie Finnis, Leslie Johns, Edna Knowles, Mrs H. Hodgson, Robert Pearson, Picturepoint Ltd., Harry Smith, and C. Williams.

index

Abbreviations:
b = black & white illustrations
p = colour illustrations
d = line drawings

129